"In an age when women are told f̲ following your feelings, our dear friends Carolyn Whitacre have mined the riches of Ecclesiastes to show us that women who are truly free 'fear God, enjoy his gifts, and anticipate his future judgment.' In their new book, *True Life*, they give us biblically rooted, Christ-exalting, and eminently practical ways to walk through the inevitable uncertainties and sorrows of 'life under the sun' with faithfulness, thoughtfulness, and joy. Brimming with a bold and God-drenched realism, *True Life* will serve any woman in any season of life."

**Bob and Julie Kauflin,** Director, Sovereign Grace Music; Pastor, Sovereign Grace Church, Louisville, Kentucky; author, *Worship Matters* and *True Worship*; and his wife

"This wise book helps us realistically assess our short life 'under the sun,' and it encourages us to fear God and to enjoy the life he has ordained for us."

**Andy and Jenni Naselli,** Associate Professor of Systematic Theology and New Testament, Bethlehem College and Seminary; Pastor, Bethlehem Baptist Church, Minneapolis, Minnesota; and his wife

"When I was twenty years old, I wondered why the book of Ecclesiastes was in the Bible. By age thirty-five it had become precious to me, as it has for countless saints through the ages. This wonderful book will help you see why. Bursting with practical counsel from 'the Preacher,' Carolyn and Nicole will help you discover the path to joy as you sojourn through the 'unhappy business' of life (Eccles. 1:13)."

**Jon Bloom,** Cofounder and teacher, Desiring God

*True Life*

# True Life

*Practical Wisdom from the Book of Ecclesiastes*

Carolyn Mahaney and
Nicole Whitacre

**CROSSWAY**®

WHEATON, ILLINOIS

Trade paperback ISBN: 978-1-4335-5251-9
ePub ISBN: 978-1-4335-5254-0
PDF ISBN: 978-1-4335-5252-6
Mobipocket ISBN: 978-1-4335-5253-3

---

**Library of Congress Cataloging-in-Publication Data**

Names: Mahaney, Carolyn, 1955- author. | Whitacre, Nicole, 1976- author.
Title: True life : practical wisdom from the book of Ecclesiastes / Carolyn Mahaney, Nicole Whitacre.
Description: Wheaton, Illinois : Crossway, 2023. | Includes index.
Identifiers: LCCN 2022018604 (print) | LCCN 2022018605 (ebook) | ISBN 9781433552519 (trade paperback) | ISBN 9781433552526 (pdf) | ISBN 9781433552533 (mobi) | ISBN 9781433552540 (epub)
Subjects: LCSH: Bible. Ecclesiastes—Criticism, interpretation, etc. | Life--Biblical teaching. | Christian women--Religious life.
Classification: LCC BS1475.52 .M27 2023 (print) | LCC BS1475.52 (ebook) | DDC 223/.806—dc23/eng/20220818
LC record available at https://lccn.loc.gov/2022018604
LC ebook record available at https://lccn.loc.gov/2022018605

---

Crossway is a publishing ministry of Good News Publishers.

BP       32   31   30   29   28   27   26   25   24   23
15   14   13   12   11   10   9   8   7   6   5   4   3   2   1

*To Kristin and Janelle—*

*Daughters, sisters, and best of friends,*
*with whom we are blessed*
*to walk through this Ecclesiastes world.*

# Contents

# Introduction

## True Life

IF WE COULD GIVE one piece of advice to every girl on the eve of graduation, every new wife or soon-to-be mother, every young Christian woman with her feet in the starting blocks of this adventure we call "life," it would be: *read the book of Ecclesiastes*. This may sound like strange advice, and Ecclesiastes is, to be fair, a strange book. But if you are "in the days of your youth," then the second-wisest man to ever live wrote it just for you (Eccles. 12:1). He wrote it to tell young people what you can expect to get out of life and how to truly live.

Find Ecclesiastes when you are older, as the two of us did, and it explains a lot. You learn that life didn't go sideways, it was already crooked (Eccles. 1:15). You realize that all your perplexing questions and confusing experiences really are mysterious, because God made them that way (Eccles. 3:11). Whatever your age, Ecclesiastes diagnoses life's ills and shows you how to enjoy life anyway.

When someone mentions Ecclesiastes, maybe you think of the opening cry of despair: "Vanity of vanities! All is vanity" (Eccles.

1:2). For many early morning Bible readers, these words prompt some head-scratching; they start searching for a more cheerful and less confusing passage for their devotions. Or perhaps you have heard this excerpt from Solomon's famous poem read aloud at a funeral: "A time to be born, and a time to die" (Eccles. 3:2). Beyond that, Ecclesiastes is one of those Old Testament books that we sometimes give a wide berth on our way to the Gospels. But while Ecclesiastes may seem confusing at first, it actually makes sense of much of life's confusion.

Solomon's book contains poetry, snippets of homespun wisdom, and grim exposés on life in the real world, all punctuated with delightful descriptions of the good life. And then at the end of life—death. Ecclesiastes talks a lot about death. Oh, and after death—judgment. Ultimately, Ecclesiastes shows us the fear of the Lord and precisely how it leads us into happy living. While there's no fabric softener or fine sugar-coating, Ecclesiastes is actually a book about joy and how to find it. Solomon explicitly states that in writing Ecclesiastes, he "sought to find words of delight" (Eccles. 12:10).

## All of Life for All of Us

Ecclesiastes is a word in season for women in every season. This is not a niche book about a specific problem; it takes in *all of life for all of us*. Ecclesiastes is for the young woman who wants to make a difference in the world for Christ and the same young woman (five years later) who feels like she is only ever changing diapers. It offers counsel for the single woman whose hopes for marriage diminish with each passing year. And it teaches the middle-aged woman—who is caring for her

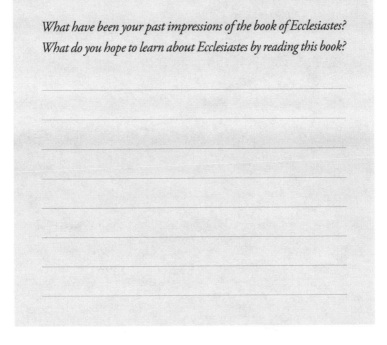

*What have been your past impressions of the book of Ecclesiastes? What do you hope to learn about Ecclesiastes by reading this book?*

elderly mother-in-law and waiting for a text from her daughter at college—how to keep running well.

You see, much of our trouble comes from the fact that we misunderstand the way life truly is. We expect that if we have enough heart and ambition we can achieve our highest goals, only to be confused and disillusioned when our plans go belly-up. *This isn't the way my life was supposed to go!* we cry. To which Solomon tells us, with a shake of his head: this is *exactly* the way life goes. It's not our life that's gone off the rails but our expectations. We are the ones who got it wrong, who mistakenly thought the "bus of life" was headed on a garden tour instead of into a war zone.

*In what ways has life gone differently from what you expected or planned?*

In Ecclesiastes, Solomon forces us to face reality. He insists—for the sake of our joy—that we reckon with the way things really are, not the way we want them to be. His goal is to free us from our illusions, and so he gives us the facts about life, straight up: "Uprightly he wrote words of truth" (Eccles. 12:10). If we believe his words of truth about the way life really is, we can learn to truly live.

"It has been said," writes J. I. Packer, "that the Psalms teach us how to worship; Proverbs, how to behave; Job, how to suffer; Song of Solomon, how to love; and Ecclesiastes, how to live."[1] Ecclesiastes gives us the wisdom we need to endure life's hardships and enjoy life's pleasures. Solomon isn't offering a free pass around troubled terrain, but he helps us avoid the pitfalls of bitterness and confusion that come from unrealistic expectations of what we can achieve. He gives us a map of life's topography so we can navigate it bravely and with a smile. Life, explains Solomon, is out of our control and beyond our comprehension. So how, then, do we truly live? The answer is to fear God, enjoy his gifts, and anticipate his future judgment.

Ecclesiastes is a realistic look behind the scenes of life. And whom do we find there? God. In all of the side roads, rabbit trails, riddles, and rants of Ecclesiastes we find our beautiful, mysterious, sovereign, and holy God. The book itself testifies that these are words from God, the "one Shepherd" (Eccles. 12:11). And because all Scripture testifies to Jesus, Ecclesiastes ultimately points to Christ as the revelation of the wisdom of God (John 5:39; 1 Cor. 1:24).

### Warming to Ecclesiastes

We began studying Ecclesiastes over a decade ago, thanks to the writings of J. I. Packer: "I warm to Ecclesiastes as a kindred spirit," he would tell people.[2] Ecclesiastes was his favorite book of the Bible, and since then it has become ours as well. Solomon's little book has taught us how not to be so surprised by life's trouble and how to laugh at the days to come (Prov. 31:25). And while life has only gotten harder in the past ten years, we have never been happier thanks to the wisdom of Ecclesiastes. In other words, Ecclesiastes has made us happy, hopeful realists. We want you to be happy, hopeful realists too, so we wrote this book about the book of the Bible that taught us how to enjoy life with God. This book is not a commentary but a testimony—which is, in fact,

*Meditate on these verses from Scripture and consider how Ecclesiastes bears witness to Christ.*

All Scripture is breathed out by God and profitable for teaching, for reproof, for correction, and for training in righteousness. (2 Tim. 3:16)

You search the Scriptures because you think that in them you have eternal life; and it is they that bear witness about me. (John 5:39)

For Jews demand signs and Greeks seek wisdom, but we preach Christ crucified, a stumbling block to Jews and folly to Gentiles, but to those who are called, both Jews and Greeks, Christ the power of God and the wisdom of God. (1 Cor. 1:22–24) what Ecclesiastes also is: a first person account of the grace of God through his written word.

In twelve short chapters, Solomon shows us how to *see* life and how to *live* it to the full. But to learn how to really live the Ecclesiastes way, we have to learn how to think like Solomon, "the Preacher" (Eccles. 1:1). Prepare yourself for a mental and emotional renovation project. Solomon's perspective on life is contrary to many of our dearest beliefs and pet values, so this will be more than a weekend job. Time is needed, which is why we have included questions for further reflection throughout each chapter. In our experience, remodeling our lives to Ecclesiastes specifications was something we had to take the time to do and then do again and again on a regular basis. But it is more than worth the effort.

We hope, by the end of this study, you'll feel the same as Martin Luther, who writes of Ecclesiastes that "this noble little book" should be "read of all . . . with great carefulness every day."[3] Long after you have put down our book, we hope you will continue to read the book of Ecclesiastes for your joy.

The words of the Preacher, the son of David, king in Jerusalem.

Vanity of vanities, says the Preacher,
vanity of vanities! All is vanity.

ECCLESIASTES 1:1–2

# 1

# Life Is Uncontrollable

WHEN NICOLE'S CHILDREN were little, they loved riding in the special grocery store cart with the car attached to the front. Tori and Sophie would clamber into the little car with all the enthusiasm of a couple of sixteen-year-olds sporting newly minted licenses. They loved feeling all grown-up, having a job to do; and they did it with gusto. Their chubby hands gripped the wheel. Their arms, like a pair of pistons, pumped incessantly. Big smiles illuminated their little faces. They reveled in the illusion that they were steering Mommy for once, turning the car this way and that, up and down the aisles.

Sometimes we have the same idea, driving through life in our brightly colored cars with shiny plastic wheels. We think we're steering this life thing pretty well, carefully turning down one aisle after another, all according to our plans. Then life veers down the cat litter aisle when we were aiming for the candy aisle. We're puzzled and dismayed: *I never meant to go* that *direction! What's happening? What did I do wrong? Why isn't life going the way I planned?*

In Ecclesiastes, it's as if Solomon leans his head down, taps the top of the little car, and speaks a few words of truth into our ideas about life in the real world. Life, he explains, is a bit like trying to steer the toy car on the front of the grocery cart. You may think that you're in control, but in reality you're not. Solomon gets straight to the point: "Vanity of vanities, says the Preacher, vanity of vanities! All is vanity" (Eccles. 1:2).

Solomon tells us what navigating life is really like for *everyone*, no exceptions. It is all vanity for all y'all. And not just vanity, but *vanity of vanities*, like the Holy of Holies or Song of Songs. The phrase uses superlative language, the ancient equivalent of an all-caps text. Then Solomon completes the triad: "All is vanity." Nothing is *not* vanity. In fact, he repeats the word for "vanity" no fewer than thirty-eight times in Ecclesiastes, and he concludes the book with the same phrase, forming a kind of frame for the entire work. In other words: "Get this! It's my main point!"

## Incomprehensible and Uncontrollable

The English word "vanity" doesn't capture all that Solomon is saying here. The word in Hebrew is *hevel*. It means "vapor" or "breath." Merest of breaths. It is, in effect, "the waste product of breathing."[1] It's the air you expel when you exhale. You even push a breath out when you say the word aloud. *Hevel*. That's life. It's the air you send out into the atmosphere. Invisible, expendable, ephemeral. Not even a yawn. So to read it properly you might say: "Merest breath, said the Preacher, merest breath. All is mere breath."[2]

We certainly don't think of our lives as a mere breath. A journey or a battle or an adventure? *Sure*. But a breath? Hardly the metaphor we would have chosen to represent the meaning and significance of

*Nothing is not vanity. Make a list of five of the most important things in your life: relationships or possessions, goals or talents—whatever comes to mind.*

1. _____

2. _____

3. _____

4. _____

5. _____

*Now turn each one into a sentence of Solomonic wisdom:*

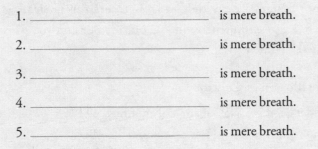

1. _____ is mere breath.

2. _____ is mere breath.

3. _____ is mere breath.

4. _____ is mere breath.

5. _____ is mere breath.

*While this exercise may seem morbid at first, we need to press in to Solomon's main point if we are to become happy, hopeful realists.*

our lives. "Vaporous!" certainly doesn't resonate or inspire. There's nothing heart-warming about the idea of life as a mere emission of carbon dioxide. And yet, this is the picture Solomon gives us.

Here's the thing about a breath: try as you might, you can't grasp it. You can't hold onto it, not even for a second. Like your physical beauty, which is "vain"—there's that word *hevel* again—you can't keep it (Prov. 31:30). A mere breath is not a thing you can grasp *tangibly* and clutch between your hands. And you cannot grasp it *intellectually* either. What does the breath we exhale mean anyway? What is the significance of a sigh? How many breaths will we take in our lifetime? There's no way we can possibly plan or decide or know. Breath eludes us, as does all of life. In other words, life is incomprehensible and uncontrollable. It's beyond our ability to understand or manage. This is reality. We can't seize the wheel of life and steer our own course with the top down and the wind in our hair. Neither can we explain life with a string of clever memes. Like a toddler in a grocery car, navigating life is beyond our comprehension and outside our control. This is the way life truly is.

**The Illusion of Control**

Evidence of our lack of control abounds, whether we realize it or not. Think about it: How often does life go contrary to what you expect or plan? You believe God helped you find a great house in a great neighborhood, only you couldn't sell your current home, and the contract fell through. The new guy at church seems godly, and maybe even interested in you, but then he asked your roommate out on a date. Perhaps you worked hard to get a small business off the ground, only for it to go under despite your best efforts. Or you tried to give all your children the same affection and opportunities, but one of them still struggles to make his way in the world.

Most of us don't interpret setbacks and reversals as Solomon did. When things don't go the way we planned or hoped, we're confused or disconsolate. But how should we think about disappointments, really? Solomon says the ability to manage the outcome of your work, relationships, and circumstances was never in your control in the first place. All the times things *did* go the way you planned were only your illusion of control. You only *thought* you were managing things while, like the child in the grocery car, you have no real control over the direction your life takes. Not a pleasant thought at first, but it is reality. Everything is *hevel*, remember? It's a breath.

---

*"What is your life? For you are a mist that appears for a little time and then vanishes."* JAMES 4:14

---

**The Default Setting: Brief, Baffling, Bad**

Years ago, slander and false accusations wreaked havoc on our family and ministry. Godly reputations were destroyed, Christian fellowship was broken, and the slander laid waste to years of fruitful ministry. At the time, we thought our lives might as well have careened off the road and plunged over a cliff. But our expectations of the way life was supposed to go needed to be adjusted. Our illusion that we could manage life (if we worked hard and obeyed God), or that we could figure it all out (if we diligently searched the Scriptures and got counsel from other believers), needed to be stripped away. Ecclesiastes brought us the comfort of knowing

*Physical beauty is* hevel. *Even if you have it, you can't hold on to it for long. As with beauty, so it is with life. What else in your life this past year has been "like a breath"—impossible to hold on to or keep?*

_____

_____

_____

_____

_____

_____

*Life is not only uncontrollable, it is incomprehensible too. Even if we think we have it all figured out, our sense of clarity can evaporate in a moment. Is there anything about your life that you are confused about today?*

_____

_____

_____

_____

_____

_____

that our experience was not unique to the Christian. The fact is: all of life is vanity for all of us.

Trouble and trials, envy and betrayal, setbacks and sorrow are all part of the treacherous terrain we travel through life on our way to death. Brief, baffling, and bad are *normal* conditions for life's journey. We can't control how long or short our lives will be; we can't fathom why things do or don't happen the way they do; and we can't take a detour around life's hazardous roads. The unexpected is exactly what we should expect from life here, in Solomon's words, "under the sun" (Eccles. 1:3).

## Stop Making Life So Hard on Yourself

We hope you can begin to see the relevance of this little book of the Old Testament. In Ecclesiastes, Solomon breaks into our frantic and futile efforts to control the uncontrollable, to comprehend the incomprehensible, and he gives us some advice: life is gonna be hard, so stop making it so hard on yourself. What is the point, Solomon asks, of trying to control people and circumstances when your life is a mere breath? What is the point of gripping the wheel so tightly when it is not connected to the tires?

Only when you recognize that life is incomprehensible and uncontrollable can you actually enjoy the ride through the grocery store of life. You can sit back and relax, turn the wheel for fun if you like! Take in the variety of cereals and pastas, enjoy exotic fruits like kumquats and kiwis or the smells of cinnamon and rye. Anticipate the goodness of God around every corner, and rest in his providence over all. He knows where you are going and why you are going there. He is in control. And that is enough.

*Read Romans 8:20–28. The apostle Paul also understood that life is vanity. In fact, the word translated as "futility" in verse 20 is the Greek equivalent of the Hebrew* hevel. *How does Paul point us to hope as we "groan inwardly" (v. 23) in this vain world?*

_____

_____

_____

_____

_____

_____

_____

_____

What does man gain by all the toil
    at which he toils under the sun?
A generation goes, and a generation comes,
    but the earth remains forever.
The sun rises, and the sun goes down,
    and hastens to the place where it rises.
The wind blows to the south
    and goes around to the north;
around and around goes the wind,
    and on its circuits the wind returns.
All streams run to the sea,
    but the sea is not full;
to the place where the streams flow,
    there they flow again.
All things are full of weariness;
    a man cannot utter it;
the eye is not satisfied with seeing,
    nor the ear filled with hearing.
What has been is what will be,
    and what has been done is what will be done,
    and there is nothing new under the sun.
Is there a thing of which it is said,
    "See, this is new"?
It has been already
    in the ages before us.
There is no remembrance of former things,
    nor will there be any remembrance
of later things yet to be
    among those who come after.

ECCLESIASTES 1:3–11

2

# Life Is Wearisome

CAROLYN'S MOTHER LIKED to tell the story about her brother's first side-hustle. Not yet old enough to earn a wage, this enterprising young man looked close to home for ways to turn a profit. He approached his two younger sisters with a business proposition: "If you give me your skinny old worthless dimes, I'll give you my big, shiny new nickels in return. What do you think?" His sisters thought this was a fabulous deal, and the young man pocketed a 50-percent return on his first investment.

Solomon has a business question for us here in the third verse: "What does man gain by all the toil at which he toils under the sun?" (Eccles. 1:3). In other words, what kind of return do we get here on earth from a lifetime investment of work and toil? What do all our efforts and all our achievements truly amount to in the end? The answer is rhetorical, of course: *Nothing*. We get nothing out of this deal of a lifetime. Here in this vain life there is no profit to be made, no edge or advantage to be gained. That's because "under the sun" (another one of Solomon's favorite phrases) all of our lives are bound by time, subject to the way things really are: uncontrollable and incomprehensible.

Toil for gain, Solomon wants us to understand, is like swapping dimes for nickels. No matter how hard we work, no matter how much effort we put into this life, we will only end up with a loss. Christian and non-Christian alike, we will have nothing left over, no profit to speak of in this life.

### Going Nowhere but Making Excellent Time

To illustrate, Solomon scans the panorama of creation in this, his first poem (Eccles. 1:2–11). What, he asks, do the sun or the wind or the streams gain from all their toil (Eccles. 1:5–7)? Just like all of us, creation is working hard with no progress to show at the end of the day. The sun rises and sets, and then rushes to do it all again tomorrow (Eccles. 1:5). The wind goes around in circles but never arrives (Eccles. 1:6). The streams work tirelessly to fill up the sea and yet never finish their job (Eccles. 1:7). All things—the sun, the wind, the water, *and our lives*—are full of weary repetition, a weariness so profound that it is beyond speech. This is the way life truly is, "For the creation was subjected to futility" (Rom. 8:20).

It's doubtful another poem has been written that so perfectly captures the day-to-day life of a mother with young children. Just like the sun, you hustle for a good spot in the carpool line only to do the same the next day. Like the streams, you load the dishwasher, only to empty it again; you fill up little bellies at breakfast that need refilling by lunchtime. And you might as well join the wind in its circuitous game of chase, for all your circling around the house to pick up toys. By the end of the day, your tank is empty; the only thing you are full of is unutterable weariness. As the old adage goes: "A mother's work is never done." But even if you don't have small children, you know the bone-weary feeling of endless repetition. Go to work, come home, go to church, come home, run errands, come home. Rinse and repeat. The wind and the sun and the streams will do it all again tomorrow, and so will you. We're all going nowhere but making excellent time. "All things are full of weariness; a man cannot utter it" (Eccles. 1:8).

Day after day we perform a litany of repetitive tasks, but Solomon pushes us to think about the end result. What are we trying to get out of life, and is it really attainable? Most of us seek satisfaction in things here under the sun. We may try to find happiness in big things such as marriage, motherhood, friendship, financial security, an impressive title or an advanced degree; or we may seek gratification in small things like a free weekend, a clean house, or a vacation. Whatever our aim, we grasp for a sense of control over some aspect of our lives that we think will bring us rest and satisfaction. But we are never totally, completely, 100 percent fulfilled. As Solomon observes, "The eye is not satisfied with seeing, nor the ear filled with hearing" (Eccles. 1:8).

Most of the time, satisfaction is just out of reach. In the words from the musical *Annie*, "It's only a day away." So close, and yet never within our grasp. Think about it. Have you ever completed your to-do list, accomplished your goals, and successfully managed your relationships, *all* in the same day? Even if we catch up on all the laundry—washed, folded, and put away—the playroom may still be a wreck. We may finally finish a big project, only to feel like we've lost touch with a dear friend. It seems there is always one child or grandchild who is struggling or suffering, who needs an extra dose of our help and prayer. As Carolyn recently told a mother who was going through a rough patch with one of her children while another of her children was thriving: "That's Ecclesiastes!"

In one way or another, we all chase that elusive moment of gratification where we can put up our feet, look around at all we have worked for, and be satisfied in our accomplishments. But that moment never comes. Instead, we are always rushing, always filling in the gaps, always striving for a better life but never arriving. We are always dissatisfied. Can you see it now? asks Solomon. You chase and strive after all the things that seem necessary for a good life under the sun, but what do you gain? Satisfaction is not on the menu of life. We will never arrive, never be completely happy and fulfilled, and that is why *all* things—sun, wind, streams, and women—are full of unutterable weariness. There is no breaking out of this weary cycle.

## Becoming a Nobody, Just Like Everybody Else

Not only is our work repetitive and full of weariness, our work itself is a repeat. Look at all the people coming and going, Solomon tells us: "A generation goes, and a generation comes" (Eccles. 1:4). Just as the sun and wind and streams go unceasingly round and round, we human beings come and go with the same uninspiring rhythm. All our productivity, all our innovations and improvements, are imitations of work that's been done before and will be done again—maybe better, maybe worse, but it hardly matters. For, in Solomon's famous words: "There is nothing new under the sun" (Eccles. 1:9). New is just a different old here on planet earth.

*Which day this past week left you feeling the most weary and exhausted? What happened to make it such a tiring day?*

_____

_____

_____

_____

_____

_____

*Solomon wants us to realize that this is the way life truly is under the sun. The Bible is nothing if not realistic. Once we learn to accept weary repetition as a fact of life, we can learn how to enjoy our tiresome toil.*

Solomon's poem runs counter to the "you are important" message that so many of us are taught as children. We are often told that we have a unique, highly specialized, and essential purpose in life, and that finding our purpose will make us feel significant and complete. And so we try to find significance in our skills, our relationships, our sacrifices, or our successes. We desire to be needed, special, or indispensable to at least a few people. Sorry to break it to you, says Solomon, but you might as well give it up, because no amount of effort and no grand endeavor will help you achieve lasting significance in this world. You're just one of a few billion people taking your turn around the track of life.

### Forgetting Forebears and Fourth Birthday Parties

Lest we think we've gamed the system and grabbed a little bit of significance in our corner of the world, Solomon tells us that our "significant" work won't be remembered at all. "There is no remembrance of former things" (Eccles. 1:11). Just as a child, when he is grown, forgets the hours of work you put into his fourth birthday party, so everyone will soon forget all that we accomplished or the difference we made in others' lives. You may be *the* church servant or the glue that holds an extended family together, you may be a standout community leader or think you are making your mark as a homemaker, health-care worker, teacher, or artist, but as one author puts it: "Achievement does not last; the mark one makes on the world is soon erased."[1]

It's been a decade now since Carolyn's parents, Ezra and Margaret, both passed away, but in that short span of time, most of what they worked for has either been removed or forgotten. A few years ago, the small, brick rambler that Carolyn's father built and that her mother cared for was demolished to make room for a new hole on the country club golf course. Even in the church where Ezra and Margaret served tirelessly for forty years, only a handful of parishoners still remember their names. Their work, though faithful and unflagging, is largely unremembered here on earth. The reality is: each of us will pass away soon. Not long after we are gone, the few people who remember what we accomplished or who appreciated our work will follow us into oblivion. A new generation will come along that knows nothing about all we overcame or achieved or gave to others.

But even while we are still alive, we are already beginning to be forgotten. As we've been writing this chapter, Carolyn has been sorting through old boxes of mementos following a recent move. When she came across her high school yearbook, she laughed to discover that she had forgotten half of the people in her small graduating class. Friends who were once so significant in her life had faded from her memory. No doubt many of them have forgotten her as well. We're so surprised to be forgotten or to forget someone who once meant so much to us. But here in Ecclesiastes, Solomon tells us that this is the way life truly is. There is no lasting significance we can attain or maintain here under the sun. Sooner or later, we're all nothing more than a fuzzy memory or a faded yearbook picture.

You see, life is a stage, and people are coming and going so often that we won't be here long enough for a curtain call. We're all "has beens" before we even get to be, and all too often what we have done has been forgotten before we're gone. Even if we are one of the few people whose exploits are recorded in history books, what advantage is that to us? We will be dead. This, says Solomon, is what's going to happen to all our labors under the sun. They will get lost in the grand, ever-growing heap of unremembered former things.

*In what areas of your life do you feel dissatisfied?*

_____

_____

_____

_____

_____

*In what ways are you striving for success?*

_____

_____

_____

_____

*How can you get off the ceaseless treadmill of satisfaction and success under the sun?*

_____

_____

_____

_____

_____

Do you feel it yet? Solomon's poem knocks the wind out of us. He wants to leave us gasping for breath so we will stop *grasping* for breath. He scorches us with the sunburn of reality so we'll have to pay attention to what life is really like under the sun. In short, we make no profit in return for all the hard work of a lifetime. All the toil at which we toil will gain us precisely nothing (Eccles. 1:3). We strive for total satisfaction and get nothing but unutterable weariness; we seek lasting significance only to end up unremarkable and unremembered. If this is the way life truly is, then do you really think you should waste it hustling after the swindle of satisfaction and significance under the sun? Take a breather, says Solomon, and listen to me for a while. I've got a better way to live.

---

*"If we work for ourselves and our own glory, it is like building our own foundation with wood or hay or straw. It will not last. But if we build for the sake of our God, it's like building a medieval cathedral: our names might be forgotten by man, but our names and our work will be remembered by God. Our work under the sun: nothing new, nothing remembered. But our work in and through the Son: something very new. It is significant, substantial—something that will be remembered and even rewarded."*[2] DOUGLAS SEAN O'DONNELL

---

*Think about your great-grandparents. How much do you know about what they accomplished in their lives? Even if a few facts do survive, most of what they achieved has probably been forgotten in only a generation or two. But what about the work we do for the Lord—isn't that supposed to last? Read 1 Corinthians 3:9–14. Consider how you can give yourself to lasting work today.*

_____

_____

_____

_____

_____

_____

_____

_____

_____

_____

I the Preacher have been king over Israel in Jerusalem. And I applied my heart to seek and to search out by wisdom all that is done under heaven. It is an unhappy business that God has given to the children of man to be busy with. I have seen everything that is done under the sun, and behold, all is vanity and a striving after wind.

What is crooked cannot be made straight,
and what is lacking cannot be counted.

ECCLESIASTES 1:12−15

3

# Life Is Unhappy

GOD MAKES HIS first appearance in Ecclesiastes 1:13 as the giver of all this weary and forgettable work we've been reading about in Solomon's poem. *God has given* us an unhappy business to be busy with. In other words, he's given us a whole lot of toil for a whole lot of nothing. What? This is not the kind of gift we expect from a good God. But that's what it says, right here in the opening verses of Ecclesiastes. All our broken relationships and disappointed dreams, all our unmet goals and dead-end efforts? "Yep, that's me," God says. "*I* have given you this unhappy business to be busy with." As Derek Kidner writes, "It is God who has prescribed the frustrations we find in life."[1]

It all started back in Genesis 3, where God first lays a curse on man's work, on "all the toil at which he toils" (Eccles. 1:3). Because you sinned, God tells Adam, "cursed is the ground because of you; in pain you shall eat of it all the days of your life; thorns and thistles it shall bring forth for you" (Gen. 3:17–18). There it is: God has given us a life of pain with no gain. A life of toil with no return. And there are no exemptions from this unhappy business, not even for Christians.

The curse is for all mankind, but the curse is not for all alike. God gave an unhappy business to men and women in their particular spheres of labor and love. While Adam and all male descendants are cursed in their work to lead and provide and subdue the earth, we as women are cursed in marriage and mothering. "In pain you shall bring forth children" (Gen. 3:16). Actually, the pain in childbirth is only just the beginning, for the discomfort in bringing them forth often fades in comparison to the heartache in bringing them up. Pregnancy can paint stretch marks across a woman's body and teenagers can carve worry lines across her face. Also, in marriage, "your desire shall be contrary to your husband, but he shall rule over you" (Gen. 3:16). In other words, a wife may try to manipulate and control her husband and a husband may tend to be harsh and overbearing with his wife. In all these ways and more, marriage and motherhood multiply wearying labors without gain. And singleness, when a woman desires marriage and motherhood, is its own kind of unhappy business.

**An Unexpectedly Unhappy Business**

Our problem is that we don't expect life to be full of unhappy business. We believe in the curse, of course, but we often underestimate what it means to live in a sin-cursed world. We may expect that as Christians, we should be exempt from the harsher realities of life under the sun. We say things like, "I had no idea motherhood would be so exhausting!" or "I never expected communication with my husband to be so exasperating!" or "I never

*The apostle Paul echoes Solomon's view of the reality of marriage and motherhood in a fallen world: "Those who marry will have worldly troubles" (1 Cor. 7:28). How have you experienced "an unhappy business" in your family life this past week?*

thought I would still be single." We forget that life really is cursed, right here where we live.

We assume that if we work hard and make wise choices, our plans and efforts will succeed. And so, when we study hard for a test and don't get a good grade, or when we take a job that doesn't work out, or when we invest our efforts in a ministry that fizzles, or when our grown-up children drift away, we're shocked, dismayed, and despondent. "Why does everything go wrong when I'm doing all the right things?" To which Solomon replies: because all your business here on earth is an unhappy business. "For that is how it is in this life," comments the ever realistic Martin Luther, "that we should expect evil things daily."[2] We should expect parenting challenges and coworker difficulties and financial setbacks and scheduling headaches . . . and the list goes on. This is the way life really is. All our days are full of unhappy business to be busy with.

Therefore do not be anxious about tomorrow, for tomorrow will be anxious for itself. Sufficient for the day is its own trouble. (Matt. 6:34)

*Ironic as it may seem, Jesus is telling us that expecting trouble today should help us not be anxious about trouble tomorrow. How does a realistic view of life help us put off the sin of anxiety?*

_____

_____

_____

_____

_____

_____

_____

## Untroubling Our Trouble

When we truly believe that God has given us an unhappy business to be busy with, it recalibrates the way we approach all our projects and pursuits. Instead of being so surprised by friction, frustration, and failure, we can learn to expect our allotted dose of daily trouble. We stop expecting things to always get better. We aren't thrown so off balance when things go from bad to worse. Unrealistic expectations "trouble our own trouble,"[3] but if we adjust our expectations to biblical realities, we can steady our souls.

What is the biblical reality? All through Scripture, God's people affirm that their unhappy business has been sent by God. And, even more strongly, they affirm that God is always at work for the good of his people (Rom. 8:28–29). As Puritan Thomas Watson writes:

> It is one heart-quieting consideration, in all the afflictions that befall us, that God hath a special hand in them: "The Almighty hath afflicted me" (Ruth 1:21). . . . Whoever brings an affliction to us, it is God that sends it. Afflictions work for good. "It is good for me that I have been afflicted" (Ps. 119:71). Joseph's brethren throw him into a pit; afterward they sell him; then he is cast into prison; yet all this did work for his good: his abasement made way for his advancement; he was made the second man in the kingdom. "Ye thought evil against me, but God meant it unto good" (Gen. 50:20). . . . God sweetens outward pain with inward peace. "Your sorrow shall be turned into joy" (John 16:20).[4]

When we acknowledge that God has "a special hand" in giving us our unhappy business, we can receive our singleness, marriage, or mothering difficulties with humility and even joy. In so doing, we will find that our unhappy business is less unhappy indeed.

---

*Whatever your unhappy business from this past week, remember: God sent it, and he means it for good. Ask him to fulfill his promise to turn your sorrow into joy.*

---

The wise person has his eyes in his head, but the fool walks in darkness. And yet I perceived that the same event happens to all of them. Then I said in my heart, "What happens to the fool will happen to me also. Why then have I been so very wise?" And I said in my heart that this also is vanity. For of the wise as of the fool there is no enduring remembrance, seeing that in the days to come all will have been long forgotten. How the wise dies just like the fool! So I hated life, because what is done under the sun was grievous to me, for all is vanity and a striving after wind.

I hated all my toil in which I toil under the sun, seeing that I must leave it to the man who will come after me, and who knows whether he will be wise or a fool? Yet he will be master of all for which I toiled and used my wisdom under the sun. This also is vanity. So I turned about and gave my heart up to despair over all the toil of my labors under the sun, because sometimes a person who has toiled with wisdom and knowledge and skill must leave everything to be enjoyed by someone who did not toil for it. This also is vanity and a great evil.

ECCLESIASTES 2:14–21

4

# Life Is Grievous

WHEN THE MYSTERIOUS Queen of Sheba visited Solomon, to see for herself the wealth and splendor of his kingdom, she gazed at his ivory palace, inspected his well-dressed servants, reclined at his sumptuous table, drank wine from his golden goblets, and marveled at all she surveyed: "There was no more breath in her" (1 Kings 10:5). Solomon's accomplishments were breathtaking.

Here in Ecclesiastes, Solomon tells us, "I the Preacher have been king over Israel in Jerusalem. And I applied my heart to seek and to search out by wisdom all that is done under heaven" (Eccles. 1:12–13). Solomon tried and tested all that life had to offer (and indeed it had *all* been offered to Solomon). The second-wisest man to walk this earth built houses for himself, planted vineyards, created gardens and parks, acquired herds and flocks, and collected silver and gold (Eccles. 2:4–9). He pursued every pleasure and project imaginable, and he succeeded in everything he put his hand to: "So I became great and surpassed all who were before me in Jerusalem" (Eccles. 2:9).

But when he finally stepped back and surveyed everything that the Queen of Sheba found so breathtaking, he pronounced it all *hevel*, nothing but a breath. After testing every pleasure and pursuit, Solomon turned his back on it all and "gave [his] heart up to despair" (Eccles. 2:20). Everything he had worked for? Everything he had accomplished? He hated it. "So I hated life, because what is done under the sun was grievous to me" (Eccles. 2:17). Why would Solomon act like he lost all his money in the stock market, when he was still the richest guy in the world? Even with all of life's unhappy business, why does he go so far as to say that he *hates* life? Isn't that a bit extreme?

### Death, the Great Eraser

Solomon hates life, not only because it is an unhappy business, but because of how it ends: *in death*. He knows that everything that is breathtaking about his accomplishments is already cursed, because one day soon, he will take his last breath. And we will too. Death serves up the same cafeteria slop to royalty and welfare recipients alike. "For you are dust, and to dust you shall return" (Gen. 3:19), remember? At the end of the day, we are all going six feet under: the CEO and the janitor, the grandmother with a large family and the infertile woman, the social media influencer and the soccer mom. Death evens the balance sheet for us all. "I perceived," writes

Solomon, "that the same event happens to all of them. Then I said in my heart, 'What happens to the fool will happen to me also. Why then have I been so very wise?'" (Eccles. 2:14–15). No matter what we do or don't accomplish, no matter how shrewd or foolhardy we have been, we're all going to end up dead. When our unhappy business on earth is through, death wipes the scoreboard clean. It robs the successful and the losers alike of *everything* they have pursued and pocketed under the sun. Good reason #1 to hate life: Death erases any lead you once held as a result of your toil.

No matter how much we get in life, we must leave it all to the next person in line. Solomon explained: "I hated all my toil in which I toil under the sun, seeing that I must leave it to the man who will come after me, and who knows whether he will be wise or a fool? Yet he will be master of all for which I toiled and used my wisdom under the sun" (Eccles. 2:18–19). Think about your work. You may be consumed with forming a ministry or fixing up a home, starting a business or creating a work of art. It remains to be seen how all your toil is going to turn out, but one thing you can know for certain: big or small, beautiful or blasé, you are going to have to leave it to someone else. And who knows, laments Solomon, what she will do with all your work? She may curate or shelve it, improve or destroy it, but either way it's up to her. One day, all our unhappy work will cease or persist at someone else's discretion. Good reason #2 to hate life: Death transfers all your work to someone else (and who knows if she will be qualified to look after it).

*What is one project of life work you are satisfied to have accomplished?*

_____

_____

_____

*How does the reality of death change your perspective on your life accomplishments?*

_____

_____

_____

_____

_____

_____

_____

_____

Solomon's predictions about death came true not five minutes after he expired, leaving his peaceful kingdom with all its wealth and glory to his son Rehoboam. You remember the story. Rehoboam consulted Solomon's advisers but promptly chucked them for the "new" guys, his youthful buddies, who gave him bad advice. Before you could say "Rehoboam," the entire kingdom, with the exception of the tribes of Judah and Benjamin, was torn away from Solomon's posterity for good. Oh, and as God told the two tribes through the prophet Shemaiah: "You shall not go up or fight . . . *for this thing is from me*" (1 Kings 12:24). Now where have we heard that before?

## Learning to Hate . . . for All the Right Reasons

Because death may be a ways off, we like to pretend that it doesn't have much to do with our work right now. It's not that we think we can avoid death—we know we can't—but we do think we can avoid the *implications of death* for a goodish long time yet. Nothing to get worked up about too soon. We'd rather not think about it. But what happens if we fail to face the reality of death? One wise pastor answers: "People develop idolatrous expectations of life by ignoring or discounting death."[1]

If you discount death, you may try to score happiness by being one smidge smarter or funnier or richer or prettier than the next girl. If you ignore death, you may find your identity in your job or in your ministry or in your children. But death means that nobody wins under the sun, and nobody is remembered. We're just keeping the seat warm until it's someone else's turn. The only way to loosen our death grip on life's pursuits and pleasures, says Solomon, is to stare death in the face.

Like Solomon, we must hate life. We must hate its terms and dread its end. We cannot control or comprehend anything. All our work is wearying and insignificant. It's nothing but an unhappy business to be busy with, and in the end we all die.

*In what do you find your identity?*

_____

_____

_____

_____

_____

_____

_____

*How does the reality of death reveal your "idolatrous expecta-tions" of life?*

_____

_____

_____

_____

_____

_____

_____

The more we contemplate these brutal conditions, the more we will feel a holy hatred. Life under the sun is positively hateful. No wonder Solomon exclaims: "*All is vanity and a striving after wind*" (Eccles. 2:17). We might as well try to grasp at our breath or corral the wind and lock the gate.

So why has Solomon taken us on this depressing tour of life's tiresome work? Why lead us to what appears to be a dead end of despair? From a New Testament perspective, we can better appreciate the significance of Solomon's words. Jesus tells us in the Gospels that you have to despair over life (that always ends in death) before you can truly live. Because only when we lose our life can we find it, and only when we hate it can we keep it for eternity (Matt. 16:25; John 12:25).

---

*"Grant, Almighty God, that as you constantly remind us in your word, and have taught us by so many examples, that there is nothing permanent in this world, but that the things which seem the firmest tend to ruin, and instantly fall and of themselves vanish away, when by your breath you shake your strength in which men trust—O grant that we, being really subdued and humbled, may not rely on earthly things, but raise up our hearts and thoughts to heaven, and there fix the anchor of our hope; and may all our thoughts abide there until at length, when you have led us through our course on earth, we shall be gathered into that celestial kingdom which has been obtained for us by the blood of your begotten Son. Amen."*[2] JOHN CALVIN

---

There is nothing better for a person than that he should eat and drink and find enjoyment in his toil. This also, I saw, is from the hand of God, for apart from him who can eat or who can have enjoyment? For to the one who pleases him God has given wisdom and knowledge and joy, but to the sinner he has given the business of gathering and collecting, only to give to one who pleases God.

ECCLESIASTES 2:24–26

5

# Life Is Enjoyable

WHEN HER THREE GIRLS WERE LITTLE, Carolyn took them to Florida by train to visit their grandparents. Her husband, CJ, dropped his family off at the station in the evening, but he couldn't join them due to some pressing work at home. The girls were crying because they were going to miss their daddy, and Carolyn had a sore throat and a fever and was dreading twenty-seven hours on a train followed by an entire week of managing the children without him. At the Sarasota station, Carolyn's mom picked them up, and as they were driving to her house, they noticed a man hitchhiking on the side of the road. It was CJ! He had flown down to meet them and stay the week. Turns out, the whole thing had been a surprise all along.

## When Dismal World Isn't

In Ecclesiastes, Solomon seems to have put us on the train to Dismal World. He has seen us off with a melancholy message: "Your whole life is like a warm breath on a cold morning: you can't grasp, manage, or control it. You can't get anything out of it and soon you will die and be forgotten. It's all an unhappy business. Oh, but have a great trip!" *Thanks a lot, Solomon.* Then just when things seem bleaker than the dark center of a Dickens novel, we see Solomon hitchhiking on the side of the road, wearing a broad smile.

Solomon pulls off his surprise beautifully. It turns out he was setting us up for joy all along. But first he had to disabuse us of all our wrong ideas about how to get happiness in this life. He needed us to see the hopelessness of gaining satisfaction or significance under the sun before we were ready to hear the secret to true joy: "There is nothing better for a person than that he should eat and drink and find enjoyment in his toil. This also, I saw, is from the hand of God, for apart from him who can eat or have enjoyment?" (Eccles. 2:24–25). Solomon is not offering a consolation prize here. Finding enjoyment in our food and drink and toil is not making the best of a bad situation. It is the only way to truly live. There is "nothing better"! Or, to match Solomon's enthusiasm: "It doesn't get any better than this!"

### Ordinary Gifts: Fried Eggs, Folded Laundry, and Much, Much More

But what Solomon considers "best ever!" surprises us too. When it comes to pursuing must-have stuff, epic experiences, or big accomplishments, Solomon is at his most disdainful. Those will get you nothing but sad, anxious days and sleepless nights (Eccles. 2:23). Instead, life's most enjoyable pleasures, the things that provide satisfying and sustaining happiness, are the simple, ordinary gifts of God, such as food and drink and work.

If we're honest, we don't always find enjoyment in food and drink and work, do we? In fact, work might be the *last* place we look to find enjoyment. It can be tedious and taxing, or merely a means to a biweekly paycheck. And while we do enjoy eating and drinking, all too often it's simply fuel to keep us going. But what if we were to see what Solomon sees? The simple, ordinary things in life are often the best things.

Also, notice that these are common gifts for commoners: work and food and drink are the basic blessings of life. Most of us have dishes to wash, a home to clean, people to care and work for. We have breakfast, lunch, and dinner, afternoon coffee breaks and midnight snacks. And we have these things almost all of the time. Food and drink and work are not milestone events; they are all-day, every-day blessings to enjoy. It is here that we can find pleasure, not just once in a while, but all the while. Rather than working and waiting for a few, brief, high-water marks in life (which often fail to deliver the joy we imagine), Solomon urges us to find enjoyment in the daily graces of fruitful labor and hearty meals. "Give us this day our daily bread," Jesus told us to pray (Matt. 6:11), and then receive it from the hand of God with joy.

This morning, Carolyn enjoyed a steaming cup of black coffee and a fried egg with cheese for breakfast. Then she noticed her grandson eyeing her fried egg and asked him if he wanted one. He wanted "two, please!" His broad smile and hearty thanks— "Mom-Mom, these are delicious!"—lit up the dim, early-morning kitchen. Food to enjoy and food to share. All this in only a quarter of an hour. You see, pleasure can be found in a tasty breakfast *and* in washing the breakfast dishes. Every made bed and mopped floor, every report filed and budget balanced, can be an occasion to relish. How about the fresh breeze through the open windows on carpool morning, the delight of reading your children's favorite book (for the hundredth time), or the blessing of easing your husband's troubles? In all these and many more, enjoyment can be found, at the table and in our toil. So sip your tea, knead your bread dough, fold your laundry, and enjoy.

All our toil gets us nowhere, but, oh my, would you look at where we are? We have been given a place to live, maybe even people to share it with. Nothing we do is new or remembered, but amazingly enough, we have all been given some work to do today, a purpose and a task. Life is full of unhappy business, but did we enjoy a cup of coffee this morning or a sandwich for lunch? How lovely. We can find enjoyment today, even in this sin-cursed world under the sun.

*How would you finish the sentence: "There is nothing better for a person than that he should* _____

_____ *"?*

*Does your "nothing better" fit with the Ecclesiastes idea of good gifts to enjoy from God?*

_____

_____

_____

_____

## Receive All You Can't Achieve

Here's the thing: we cannot *achieve* enjoyment; we can only *receive* it from God's hand. As Solomon explains: "This also, I saw, is from the hand of God, for apart from him who can eat or who can have enjoyment?" (Eccles. 2:24–25). Every delicious meal and cold drink, every job well done, is from the hand of God, but so is the *enjoyment* of that meal and drink and job. See, you can work hard and make a lot of money and dine at expensive restaurants, but you cannot actually get enjoyment from food or drink unless God gives it to you from his hand. You can attract the attention of a good-looking man and get married and find a nice house and have adorable children, but you cannot be happy in your work in the home apart from God giving you joy.

The reason that so many Christians fail to find enjoyment in life is that we still try to achieve more than we have received. "The basic things of life are sweet and good," acknowledges Derek Kidner. "What spoils them is our hunger to get out of them more than they can give."[1] Often we may throw ourselves into our work, not for the pleasure of fulfilling the task that God has called us to, but because we are hungry for satisfaction and significance. Mothering our children becomes about looking good to others. Starting a small business becomes about establishing a reputation for ourselves in the community. Ministry work becomes a means to an end: to get attention or respect or appreciation. Even food and drink become utilitarian, a way to keep our energy up as we pursue our selfish goals. But if we hunger after applause from others through our work, we will never be satisfied. If we are so busy chasing success, we might fail to enjoy the sweetness of family dinners or fellowship with friends over a good meal.

## The Good Giver Gives Good Gifts

Turns out, life is not at all like we thought. Life is not about reaching our dreams or fulfilling our potential or becoming the best version of ourselves. Instead, life is about receiving from the hand of God whatever he chooses to give. In short, we human beings are receivers not achievers. God has *given* us an unhappy business to be busy with (Eccles. 1:13), and now Solomon tells us that God has also *given* us joy: "For to the one who pleases him God has given wisdom and knowledge and joy" (Eccles. 2:26). God gives unhappy business, and he gives happy business. And while the unhappy business is for everyone, finding enjoyment is only for "the one who pleases him." Only those who are in Christ (with whom his Father is "well pleased") receive joy in the midst of their cursed work (Matt. 3:17).

God the giver shines out here at the end of Ecclesiastes 2. Every satisfying meal and refreshing drink, every invigorating task: all our enjoyment in all these things is from his hand. God is personal and perpetual in his generosity. But who are we to receive all good things to enjoy from God the giver? We deserve nothing from God but unhappy business. All of us were sinners who rebelled against God, grasping at his good gifts for selfish gain. But then our merciful God gave us the most extraordinary gift of all: "For God so loved the world, that *he gave his only Son*, that whoever believes in him should not perish but have eternal life" (John 3:16). Our heavenly Father gave his only Son, Jesus Christ, so that through Christ's perfect life, death, and resurrection, we can receive and enjoy God's good gifts. Truly, "He comes to make His blessings flow, far as the curse is found."[2]

Every good gift and every perfect gift is from above, coming down from the Father of lights, with whom there is no variation or shadow due to change. (James 1:17)

*Make a list and thank the Father of lights for the good and perfect gifts you have received this week:*

- _____

- _____

- _____

- _____

- _____

For everything there is a season, and a time for every matter under heaven:

a time to be born, and a time to die;
a time to plant, and a time to pluck up what is planted;
a time to kill, and a time to heal;
a time to break down, and a time to build up;
a time to weep, and a time to laugh;
a time to mourn, and a time to dance;
a time to cast away stones, and a time to gather stones together;
a time to embrace, and a time to refrain from embracing;
a time to seek, and a time to lose;
a time to keep, and a time to cast away;
a time to tear, and a time to sew;
a time to keep silence, and a time to speak;
a time to love, and a time to hate;
a time for war, and a time for peace.

What gain has the worker from his toil? I have seen the business that God has given to the children of man to be busy with. He has made everything beautiful in its time.

ECCLESIASTES 3:1–11

6

# Life Is Well-Timed

JUST AS THE FOUR SEASONS breeze in, coloring the landscape and altering the temperature, and melt away, taking deferential leave at their appointed time, so the seasons of our lives come and go, coloring and altering the landscape of our homes, tasks, emotions, and relationships. We have no control over the seasons of the year: we cannot tell summer to "start on your mark" or give winter two-week's notice, and so we adapt and plan our lives around their ever-changing patterns. Neither can we control the seasons and times of our lives. They trot in or trickle out, one after another, but all of them are beyond our control. The times of our lives—none of which we decide—is what Solomon's second, and most famous, poem is about (Eccles. 3:1–8).

## Dancing to Someone Else's Tune

Many peer at this poem the same way they look at all of life: through a self-determining filter. They think Ecclesiastes 3:1–8 is an array of options from which they can pick and choose their times and seasons. But if that were the case, who of us would choose "a time to weep," "a time to lose," or "a time for war" (vv. 4, 6, 8)? The point of Solomon's poem is that we *don't* choose our times; they are chosen for us. We don't schedule our seasons; they are predetermined: beginning, duration, and end. There is a time for everything, but *not* a time of our choosing for anything. We did not pick the day of our birth, and we will not decide the day of our death; neither can we map out life's journey or choose where we'll stop along the way. As Derek Kidner sums it up: "We dance to a tune, or many tunes, not of our own making."[1] As hard as it is for us to accept this fact, the reality is: nothing in life is self-determined.

---

*"Not only that God by his providence rules the world, and governs all things in general, but that it reaches to every detail; not only to order the great affairs of kingdoms, but it reaches to every man's family; it reaches to every person in the family; it reaches to every condition; yea to every happening, to everything that falls out concerning you in every particular: not one hair falls from your head, not a sparrow to the ground, without the providence of God. Nothing befalls you, good or evil, but there is a providence of the infinite eternal first Being in that thing; and therein is God's infiniteness, that it reaches to the least things, to the least worm that is under your feet."*[2] JEREMIAH BURROUGHS

---

The key to unlocking Solomon's poem is found under the doormat of verses 9 and 10: "What gain has the worker from his toil? I have seen the business that God has given to the children of man to be busy with" (Eccles. 3:9–10). There it is again: "*God has given.*" All of the times of living and dying, weeping and laughing, warring and peacemaking, plucking and planting? It's *all* business that God the giver has given us to be busy with. And every season—long and short, good and bad—is under his control.

## The God behind the Relationships

Look closely and you'll see that this poem also has a lot to do with people, as do our lives. Times and seasons are often set in motion, interrupted, or even redirected by our relationships. As hard as we may try to manage or influence other people, we spend most of our lives responding to the words, actions, and needs of those around us. We sit in *silence* beside a grieving friend, and *speak* a hard truth to a wayward Christian. We *laugh* at a mischievous toddler, and *weep* over a resentful teenager. We *love* righteousness, and we *hate* sin. The various seasons of our lives are affected by the changing character of our relationships. As one author poignantly illustrates: "We dance at a wedding, and we mourn the loss of the one we danced with. We laugh together, and we weep for what the people we used to laugh with have done to us."[3] But no matter how much our lives seem determined by what other people have done to us, it is God who is behind the scenes, doing it all.

God is the one giving us all this people-business to be busy with. He is the one stage-managing all the times and seasons of all the relationships in our lives. As Jonathan Edwards observes: "The fact, that the hand of God is a great deal more concerned in all that happens to us than the treatment of men is, should lead us, in a great measure, not to think of things as from men, but to have respect to them chiefly as from God."[4] God is in control of everything that people try to control or even appear to control. Whether it is a great war or a personal conflict, an accidental fire or a boss firing, a friend's care or a stranger's unkindness, we are not at the mercy of other people's actions. No matter how much a situation may appear to be from the hand of man, there is "providence . . . in that thing."[5] God is behind all of it.

Everything that happens to us is chiefly from God, and everything that happens to our loved ones is from him as well. On the same day this week, one of our family members lost his job due to layoffs while another received a long-hoped-for promotion. Remembering that the hand of God is a great deal more concerned in "a time to seek, and a time to lose" than any supervisor or coworker, any teacher or classmate, can protect us from fear and infuse us with hope as we wait for his good purposes to unfold for those we love.

## All Things Bewildering and Beautiful

Solomon's poem presents life and relationships in their complexities and complications, their reversals and renewals, their melancholies and their merrymakings, all woven together to form God's grand plan. He is above the sun, orchestrating every moment and emotion of every person's life under the sun. All the undulating times and maturing seasons fit into a perfect pattern that only he can see. When we try to make sense of it all, we can only squint at what appears to be a mass of tangled threads, incomprehensible to us. But each strand is intricately hand-stitched by God. He is fashioning this masterpiece out of all the threads of all the lives

*What situations have come your way recently that seem to be from the hand of man?*

_____

_____

_____

_____

_____

_____

*How do these verses from Ecclesiastes and the reality that these things are from "the hand of God," as Jonathan Edwards says, alter your view?*

_____

_____

_____

_____

_____

_____

of all the people who have ever lived, and he is doing it all for his glorious purposes.

We can only see a small fragment of what God is doing in our lives; the complete pattern is hidden from our view. But this passage also gives us a glimpse of what God has done, *beyond our view*: "He has made everything beautiful in its time" (Eccles. 3:11). This, as one commentary claims, is "the greatest statement of divine providence in the whole of Scripture."[6] What confidence and comfort to know that not only is God in control of everything, he is controlling everything in such a way that makes it *beautiful*! Better than that, he already *has* made it beautiful. It is already done and dusted, determined and decided, a *fait accompli*.

In God's sublime sovereignty, the times and seasons of our lives have been made beautiful before they even happen. At present, things may appear ugly, twisted, confusing, and even hopeless to us, but he has already preordained their beautiful outcome. Each and every event in our lives is not only *controlled* by God, it has been *crafted* by God with purpose, precision, grace, and glory. He has a reason for every season of our lives. Unlike us, God does nothing in vain. He has made *every single thing*—every setback, every slanderous tongue, every faithless friend, every grim diagnosis, every mistake, every parenting heartbreak, every financial loss and lack, every injustice, and every bit of bad news—to be exquisitely, breathtakingly beautiful in his time.

When we inhale the clear, clean air of God's providence that permeates this poem, our souls are refreshed. We don't need to figure out the meaning of our lives or fret over our lack of control. We are free to receive and enjoy, to work and to rest, in the comforting shadow of God's beautiful sovereignty. He's controlling it all, so go enjoy a glass of wine. He's bringing his great plan to pass, so tackle your to-do list peacefully. Solomon wants more for us than merely coping with life's changes and challenges. He wants us to truly live. To truly live, he tells us, you must *truly trust* in the sovereignty of God.

*Meditate on the perfect timing of God's beautiful plan of salvation:*

But when *the fullness of time* had come, God sent forth his Son, born of woman, born under the law. (Gal. 4:4)

For while we were still weak, *at the right time* Christ died for the ungodly. (Rom. 5:6)

Therefore, stay awake, for you do not know *on what day* your Lord is coming. (Matt. 24:42)

Also, he has put eternity into man's heart, yet so that he cannot find out what God has done from the beginning to the end. . . .

I perceived that whatever God does endures forever; nothing can be added to it, nor anything taken from it. God has done it, so that people fear before him.

ECCLESIASTES 3:11, 14

7

# Life Is Incomprehensible

EACH AND EVERY DAY, a mother parleys hundreds of questions from her toddler, only to receive "But, why?" on the rebound. Unless the curious toddler can be distracted, this fun little game may go on for an indefinite period of time. While we all eventually outgrow the pesky habit of asking "Why?" to every statement, we never outgrow the question. If anything, our desire to know why only intensifies the older we get. Mothers and toddlers alike, we all carry around this big, little question in our hearts.

## The Eternal Purpose of Everything under the Sun

Why do we ask so many "why" questions? Because, explains Solomon, God put them there. "He has put eternity into man's heart" (Eccles. 3:11). You see, as human beings created in the image of God, we realize that there must be a bigger picture to the big picture of God's sovereign rule over time and seasons. That's because God has embedded eternity in our hearts. God has made something beautiful out of everything, and everything

*While we may enjoy reading mystery novels, what we don't always enjoy is having an unsolved mystery in our lives. What is the biggest unsolved mystery in your life at present?*

he does "endures forever; nothing can be added to it, nor anything taken from it" (3:14). Unlike what we do, which must be done and redone, and rarely lasts the morning (*Moms, you know what we're talking about here!*), everything that God does stands the test of time and then forever after that. In other words, more is going on here under the sun than meets the eye. There is an eternal purpose for everything. And so we instinctively want to know more about the meaning of life and how it all fits together.

But there's a catch. God has put limits on how much we can figure out about his eternal purposes. We "cannot find out what

God has done from the beginning to the end" (Eccles. 3:11). In other words, a lot of our "why" questions bounce back with no answers because they hit the borders of our capacity to comprehend God's eternal purposes. The result is that many of the circumstances in our lives remain mysterious to us. We know that they have meaning and significance, but often we don't understand how they fit into God's overarching plan. For the same God who puts eternity in our hearts also curbs our ability to take it all in from beginning to end. Not only is God sovereign over every time and season (Eccles. 3:1–8), his sovereignty is inscrutable and incomprehensible (Eccles. 3:11). As J. I. Packer writes: God "has hidden from us almost everything that we should like to know about the providential purposes which he is working out . . . in our own lives."[1]

## When the Good Comes to a Bad End

Despite this reality, many of us still go through life assuming that God's eternal plan can be clearly understood by Christians. Because "we know that for those who love God all things work together for good, for those who are called according to his purpose" (Rom. 8:28), we expect things to turn out good for us— if not immediately, then at least eventually. Then we bump into our own seemingly senseless tragedy or loss, where no good can be found, not even after many years of hard searching. Our faith falters. Our neat and perfect answers to all the "why" questions collapse under the strain. We begin to wonder if maybe life under the sun really is meaningless after all. Things look chaotic rather than crafted, confusing rather than clear, bewildering rather than beautiful. "Not only may you see a tiny fraction of what God is doing in your life," writes John Piper, "the part you do see may make no sense to you."[2]

Elisabeth Elliot learned this difficult lesson early in her missionary work. Prior to marrying Jim Elliot, Elisabeth worked for nine months in another part of Ecuador where she studied and transcribed the language of the Colorado Indians for the purpose of translating the New Testament. The work was progressing well, when two sharp blows brought it to a sudden end. First, her only translator was murdered, then all of her linguistic notes and files were stolen, never to be recovered. Her friend was dead, and nine months of painstaking effort to translate God's word was lost. It all seemed so senseless. Elliot's biographer writes,

> The question "why?" not only remained unanswered in practical terms, it also could not be neatly resolved by the skillful rearrangement of facts to produce the proper "spiritual" answer. This death, this loss, defied the usual religious formula: *Well, this bad thing happened so God could do x, y, and z, beyond what we could have asked or imagined.*[3]

## But God Gives Himself

Like a young Elisabeth Elliot, Carolyn also thought she knew the "proper 'spiritual' answer" to her questions. When the slanderous onslaught against CJ stretched into years, however, nothing seemed to make sense. *Why did God allow her godly husband to be slandered in such a vile manner? Why did God permit such widespread damage to years of fruitful ministry? Why did God raise up so few men willing to defend the truth for the sake of the gospel?* The harder Carolyn tried to figure things out, the closer she came to the brink of despair. Every time she thought she caught a glimpse of what God might be doing, or put her hope in a fresh scenario of deliverance, or imagined she could see a beautifully fitting way this might end, things only seemed to grow more confusing and painful. The senselessness of it all was, perhaps, the most oppressive part of the whole ordeal.

It was then that God graciously led her to Ecclesiastes and these verses. Here God delivered her: not from her troubles but from the burden of trying to *understand* her troubles. Here she saw that she could not see. She figured out that she could not, and would not, be able to figure it all out. Over time, her confusion cleared and, even though the slanderous accusations continued, the oppressive weight of trying to understand why was lifted. When Carolyn realized that God had implanted in her heart *both* the longing to make sense of the situation *and* the limitations on her understanding, she was free to leave all her unanswered questions just as they were—unanswered. She learned that the only way to find peace under the burden of our unanswered questions is to accept that we cannot figure everything out. To this day, the answer to Carolyn's "why?" has never come, but she sees all that she needs to see and knows all that she needs to know.

---

*"As believers we cannot always know why, but we can always know why we trust God who knows why, and that makes all the difference."*[4] OS GUINNESS

---

"It was a long time," said Elisabeth Elliot about her unexplained losses, "before I came to the realization that it is in our acceptance of what is given that God gives Himself."[5] *This* is the eternal purpose behind our perplexities: God is leading us to himself. As Solomon explains, "God has done it, so that people fear before him" (Eccles. 3:14). All our frustrations in life are to lead us to fear God. Take your big "why" question, whatever it may be, and fill in the answer.

Why is your life this way?

Because fearing God is the way you were meant to truly live.

## Frustration in Life and the Fear of the Lord

When we finally understand that we cannot control any of the events of our lives and that we cannot comprehend them either, when—like Elisabeth and Carolyn—we realize there really is nothing we can do to fix the situation or figure things out, *then* we come to the fear of the Lord. God in his kindness has been leading us here all along. It is why he has done *everything*. God never stops working in our lives; rather, this is *how* he works. He brings us to the end of ourselves in order to bring us to himself. When we finally realize we have no alternatives and no answers, what do we do? We turn to him. We fear him. As Martin Luther comments on this verse:

> Anyone who believes . . . that matters have not been placed into our hands . . . will attribute everything to God in His working, and will expect everything from Him. If He grants it, he enjoys it; if He does not, he does without it; and if He takes it away, he bears it. . . . This is what it means to fear

God: to have God in view, to know that He looks at all our works, and to acknowledge Him as the Author of all things, both good and evil.[6]

Our inability to fix life's problems and figure out life's perplexities is meant to help us *see God*, who controls all things for

> *Consider the unsolved mystery in your life that you identified earlier. It could be a good thing (like marriage or motherhood) that you want but don't have. Or it could be someone or something good that you have lost (like a loved one). Maybe it's a difficulty or trial that you didn't expect, something you have but don't want. How does Ecclesiastes help you to turn away from your unanswered questions to the fear of God?*

all time and all eternity. We learn to fear God, to have him in view as the author of all things. He has granted every achievement, sent every trouble, and steered every unexpected turn. When we have joy, he has given it. When we have hardship, he has given that too. Whatever comes to us—good or bad—comes from him. Everything, absolutely everything, about our lives traces back to his working, and all our working and enjoying is done before him. To fear God is to live in the reality that we are under the sun and he sits above it. To fear God is to be in awe of the majesty, beauty, humility, and love of Jesus Christ. When we have God in view, our view of life is transformed, and so is the way we live.

Perhaps the fear of God isn't the answer that you were expecting. It turns out though, it's what Solomon has been driving at for three chapters now. In one sense, this verse is the big reveal. Solomon gathers everyone together and tells us what all these mysterious happenings under the sun have been about: it's all been so that we will fear before God. Or, to put it positively: fearing God is the only way to truly live. For the rest of Ecclesiastes, Solomon will continue to insist that we face reality, but he will also expand on how to truly live in light of reality, how to walk in the fear of the Lord in all our laughing and laboring under the sun. He sums up his entire purpose in the final words of his book: "The end of the matter; all has been heard. Fear God and keep his commandments, for this is the whole duty of man" (Eccles. 12:13). How do we truly live under the sun? Keep God in view. Fear before him. Obey. Not only is fearing God our whole duty, it is our highest joy.

Since God is contented with himself alone, if you have him, you may be contented with him alone, and it may be, that is the reason why your outward comforts are taken from you, that God may be all in all to you. It may be that while you had these things they shared with God in your affection, a great part of the stream of your affection ran that way: God would have the full stream run to him now.[7] JEREMIAH BURROUGHS

*Pray that God would be "all in all" to you.*

I perceived that there is nothing better for them than to be joyful and to do good as long as they live; also that everyone should eat and drink and take pleasure in all his toil—this is God's gift to man.

ECCLESIASTES 3:12–13

8

# Live Faithfully

WHEN NICOLE'S OLDEST SON, Jack, graduated from high school, he was, like many homeschoolers, a graduating class of one. And so, on a hot and sticky evening in June, the entire family gathered for a simple ceremony in the Whitacre dining room. With help from Carolyn, Nicole prepared a meal of Jack's favorite appetizers. Jack's siblings and cousins presented an original video retrospective; Jack delivered a valedictory speech; and Nicole's husband, Steve, gave the commencement address. It was a happy and memorable evening, even if the graduate did get buffalo wing hot sauce on his graduation gown.

While a high school graduation marks the end of one season, it heralds the beginning of a new and exciting time in life. Many graduates spend hours pondering, "What should I do with my life?" Some are anxious and uncertain of what to do next, while others have ambitious plans for success all mapped out. But we are not the ones with the master plan for our lives. God is. As Solomon has taken great pains to point out, we cannot control our lives, and we cannot comprehend God's overall plan.

C. S. Lewis spoke to young men just embarking on their academic careers at the beginning of World War II in his famous lecture, "Learning in War-time." When life doesn't go the way you planned, Lewis explained to these Oxford University students, the realization is meant to teach you something about the world and how to live:

> We see unmistakably the sort of universe in which we have all along been living, and must come to terms with it. If we had foolish un-Christian hopes about human culture, they are now shattered. If we thought we were building up a heaven on earth, if we looked for something that would turn the present world from a place of pilgrimage into a permanent city satisfying the soul of man, we are disillusioned, and not a moment too soon.[1]

Disillusionment, in other words, is a blessing in disguise. When we finally face life head-on—with all its grim realities—then we can come to terms with it. When we finally see life for what it truly is, we can learn how to truly live. So it's a good thing for us to have our foolish hopes shattered, because only then can we learn how to navigate life with all its hazards and headaches. This is what Solomon has been getting at all along in Ecclesiastes. He "disillusions us to bring us to reality,"[2] as Derek Kidner puts it so well. Solomon tears us down in order to build us back up again. Let's face it, says Solomon: Life is uncontrollable and incomprehensible. Live as if that were true. Now that I've got you good and disillusioned about life, he says, let me teach you how to live in the real world.

*Think about a significant or recent moment of disillusionment in your life. How can it be a moment of grace to lead you to the joy of living the Ecclesiastes way?*

## "Be Joyful" . . . Easier Done Than Said?

In all our planning and praying about our futures, Solomon tells us the best way to live, whether we are a graduate or a grandmother: "I perceived that there is nothing better for them than to be joyful and to do good as long as they live" (Eccles. 3:12). For all our times and seasons, the way to navigate life here under the sun is to be joyful and do good for as long as we live.

This job sounds like fun; we'll happily sign our names to the "be joyful" clipboard. But we're not sure how to pull it off exactly. Is being joyful something you can actually choose to do? How can we be joyful when all our plans fall apart? Here's the thing, says Solomon, joy is not something on the other side of a college scholarship or a kitchen remodel. It's not the outcome of any effort or achievement in your life. You don't finish the job or fulfill your dreams and then be joyful. You can't work to achieve joy. Being joyful *is* the job. It's the delightful task we are to fulfill today, tomorrow, and every day for the rest of our lives. It's an everyday job for every season. Which is why Solomon perceived "there is nothing better for them . . . as long as they live" (Eccles. 3:12).

How can we be joyful? By enjoying God's gifts. As Solomon reiterates: "Everyone should eat and drink and take pleasure in all his toil—this is God's gift to man" (Eccles. 3:13). Our "be joyful" job is actually quite straightforward. We simply need to look for God's ordinary gifts and enjoy them daily, as they come. "Approach life receptively," encourages one commentator, "enjoy God's good gifts as they unfold."[3] To approach life receptively we must approach each day receptively. It begins with prayer. Think back over the previous day and thank God for blessings of food and drink, work and rest, friends and family, wisdom, strength, and every answered prayer. Write them down if you like. Then ask God for more of the same gifts of grace for the new day. As you go about your day, watch for and enjoy each good gift as it comes.

No matter how diminished your current circumstances or how difficult your present road, God is giving you gifts to enjoy today. When slander engulfed her church, Carolyn created a daily list of gifts from God and shared it with her family for encouragement. They were all surprised by how many kind and gracious gifts God was giving, even in the midst of their unhappy business.

In the bad times, we don't always perceive God's gifts, and in the good times, we may forget God's benefits (Ps. 103:2). We may even assume (*gasp!*) that *we* have earned or achieved some blessing or other by our own efforts or strength. Which is why James—surely a student of Solomon—tells us, "Do not be deceived" about where good gifts come from: "Every good gift and every perfect gift is from above, coming down from the Father of lights" (James 1:16–17). Every straight-A semester and every eight-hour night of uninterrupted sleep and every dandelion bouquet from your grandson is from above, and we should enjoy it properly, as coming down from the Father of lights. When you start living life receptively, you discover that every day really is like Christmas. Makes sense then, why Solomon says, there is "nothing better . . . than to be joyful" (Eccles. 3:12).

*Psalm 100:2 tells us to "serve the LORD with gladness!" What is one way that God is calling you to serve him with joy today?*

_____

_____

_____

_____

_____

_____

## Whistle While You . . . Toil

Solomon's wisdom takes the guesswork out of what it means to truly live. Instead of following a ten-year plan—which, let's face it, doesn't usually survive the year—we should "do good" today (Eccles. 3:12). We should "take pleasure in all [our] toil—this is God's gift to man" (Eccles. 3:13). Let's be honest: toil is not usually our go-to activity for pleasure. In fact, we often think of our work as the most *un*pleasant part of our lives. But Solomon says just the opposite. Not only does God fill our lives with good to do today, he then goes and tops off all our work with pleasure. He gives us a sense of purpose in having a job to do, and he gives us pleasure in completing that job. We can find satisfaction in an empty laundry basket or email inbox, fulfillment in a restocked pantry or a completed report. God gives us joy and delight in doing good.

In fact, toil is often what gets us through the unpleasant times in life. Work is a special gift in seasons of difficulty or uncertainty. Whether we are anxious or grieving, waiting for news or faced with a big decision—there is always something good to do right in front of us. Make the bed. Do the homework. Put the laundry in the dryer. No matter how many questions fill our minds or how many tears fill our eyes, we will experience grace in simply being faithful. As Elisabeth Elliot once shared, "'Do the next thing.' I don't know any simpler formula for peace, for relief from stress and anxiety than that very practical, very down-to-earth word of wisdom. Do the next thing. That has gotten me through more agonies than anything else I could recommend."[4]

Doing the next thing also starts with prayer. Ask God, "What's next? What good do you want me to do today?" As Paul elaborates in the New Testament, "For we are his workmanship, created in Christ Jesus for good works, which God prepared beforehand, that we should walk in them" (Eph. 2:10). Often we know what good works we should walk in today. It's the duty right in front of us. Pack your husband's lunch. Feed and clean up after the toddler. Run errands. Meet a client. Visit an elderly neighbor. Study for your exams. Pray and do the next thing. But keep watch, because God is fond of handing out last-minute assignments. While he's prepared all our good works ahead of time, he doesn't always tell us what he has prepared. Messes, mess-ups, and interruptions may not be in *our* plans, but they are all part of God's beautiful plan.

Doing good may seem ordinary, mundane, and even menial, which is why we avoid it sometimes. *Surely this can't be the good God has called me to do? Doesn't God have more significant work for me to accomplish?* Many women assume they need a position or a platform before they can do any good; or, they think doing good is something they must prepare to step into someday. But we don't need to achieve an important position in order to do important work. God has prepared important good works for each of us to walk in, every day, for as long as we live. Doing good may not be glamorous but it is glorious, because it is God's gift to us. The menial becomes meaningful when God crowns it with purpose and pleasure.

### When Life Is Gift, Not Get

Whether you are a graduate with big plans for your future or a grandmother who feels like all your plans have come to nothing, Ecclesiastes recalibrates our whole way of thinking about how to truly live. There is nothing better than to be joyful and do good and so participate in God's master plan. *This is God's gift to man.* As one

*We know Dorcas in the Bible as the woman that God raised from the dead through the prayers of the apostle Peter. Scripture not only tells us how she came back to life but how she lived her life: "She was full of good works and acts of charity" (Acts 9:36). Let's pray and resolve to truly live like Dorcas.*

commentator sums it all up: "Life in God's world is gift, not gain."[5] This is the point Solomon is trying to drive home. Life is given, not grabbed. Life is receiving, not achieving. Life is an unhappy business, but God gives us food and drink to enjoy. Life is full of toil, but God gives us pleasure in our work. Life is nothing but a breath, but there is nothing better than to be joyful and do good.

From an old English parsonage down by the sea
There came in the twilight a message to me;
Its quaint Saxon legend, deeply engraven,
Hath, it seems to me, teaching from Heaven.
And on through the doors the quiet words ring
Like a low inspiration: "DO THE NEXT THING."

Many a questioning, many a fear,
Many a doubt, hath its quieting here.
Moment by moment, let down from Heaven,
Time, opportunity, and guidance are given.
Fear not tomorrows, child of the King,
Trust them with Jesus, *do the next thing.*

Do it immediately, do it with prayer;
Do it reliantly, casting all care;
Do it with reverence, tracing His hand
Who placed it before thee with earnest command.
Stayed on Omnipotence, safe 'neath His wing,
Leave all results, *do the next thing.*

Looking for Jesus, ever serener,
Working or suffering, be thy demeanor;
In His dear presence, the rest of His calm,
The light of His countenance be thy psalm,
Strong in His faithfulness, praise and sing.
Then, as He beckons thee, *do the next thing.*[6]

AUTHOR UNKNOWN

Then I saw that all toil and all skill in work come from a man's envy of his neighbor. This also is vanity and a striving after wind. The fool folds his hands and eats his own flesh. Better is a handful of quietness than two hands full of toil and a striving after wind.

Again, I saw vanity under the sun: one person who has no other, either son or brother, yet there is no end to all his toil, and his eyes are never satisfied with riches, so that he never asks, "For whom am I toiling and depriving myself of pleasure?" This also is vanity and an unhappy business.

Two are better than one, because they have a good reward for their toil. For if they fall, one will lift up his fellow. But woe to him who is alone when he falls and has not another to lift him up! Again, if two lie together, they keep warm, but how can one keep warm alone? And though a man might prevail against one who is alone, two will withstand him—a threefold cord is not quickly broken.

ECCLESIASTES 4:4–12

9

# Live Industriously

ONE OF CAROLYN'S go-to cookbooks in the early days of marriage and motherhood was the *More-with-Less Cookbook*, a collection of recipes from the Mennonite community. Although Carolyn was only a few months old when her parents left the Mennonite denomination to join another church, many of these recipes remain a part of her culinary heritage. Carolyn and her girls still make the "High Protein Rolls," "Honey Baked Chicken," and "Pancake Mix" for their families.

Solomon has a more-with-less policy when it comes to life and the work we give our lives to. We all have work to do. God has assigned us all times of sowing and reaping, building up and tearing down. But *how* we work makes all the difference in how we live. If we're going to learn how to truly live, we have to learn how to truly work. How should we work, exactly? "Better [read: Best!] is a handful of quietness," says Solomon (Eccles. 4:6). In other words, the best work is done with "contentment." Or, to put it another way: you'll get more out of life if you learn to make do with less.

Quiet work requires a little counterintuitive math: we choose one handful instead of two hands full. Or, as Jeremiah Burroughs explains: "*A Christian comes to contentment [quietness] not so much by way of addition, as by way of subtraction . . .* not by adding more to his condition; but rather by subtracting from his desires, so as to make his desires and his circumstances even and equal."[1] Quietness is being satisfied with the food and drink, the family and friends, the home and the work that God has given us, instead of straining our hearts and bending our backs trying to get more. Rather than working hard to get what our heart desires, we work hard to bring our desires down to what we already have. Make 'em nice and even. This is better.

---

"*But godliness with contentment is great gain, for we brought nothing into the world, and we cannot take anything out of the world. But if we have food and clothing, with these we will be content.*" I TIMOTHY 6:6–8

---

### Envy, a Sin That's Deadly *and* No Fun at All

The real difficulty, though, is not getting our desires equal to what we have; it is learning to be content with less than what *she* has. In fact, Solomon tells us that it is the sin of envy— the desire to have better and to be better than others—that motivates all the toil and striving under the sun. "Then I saw that all toil and all skill in work come from a man's envy of his neighbor" (Eccles. 4:4). In other words, all the vain work in all the world is motivated by "the craving to outshine or not to be outshone."[2]

You see, envy doesn't just want something—that's greed or covetousness. What envy wants is to have a *better* something than the next person, or more precisely, to *be better* than the next person. We want to outshine, or at least not be outshone; and so we toil and strive for the spotlight. We angle to get our gifts and talents recognized in church as much as the next woman. We try to make our home look more trendy than our best friend's home. We push our kids to be as successful as our neighbor's kids. And when it comes to our sister, well, we want to be better than her at everything. We don't merely desire significance and satisfaction under the sun; we want to get *more than her.*

No matter how hard envy strives—and it's a workhorse!—it always falls short of happiness, for envious people "pursue happiness in a way that necessarily undermines their own chances of having it."[3] Solomon wants us to enjoy life, and envious work, he tells us, is exactly how *not* to enjoy it. "This also is vanity and a striving after wind" (Eccles. 4:4). Because, like chasing the wind, the envier never catches what she wants, she only grows more and more discontent, less and less quiet in her work. As one author puts it: "Of the seven deadly sins, only envy is no fun at all."[4]

### Learning to Rest at the Right Time and in the Right Way

Solomon has warned us against the *wrong* kind of work—work done from envy—and now he warns us against the *wrong* kind

*Think about your work. Is there any aspect of your work in the home or in parenting or in your job that is motivated by envy?*

_____

_____

_____

_____

_____

_____

*Ask for God's forgiveness through Jesus Christ and then consider: How can you do quiet work for the Lord instead?*

_____

_____

_____

_____

_____

_____

of rest: "The fool folds his hands and eats his own flesh" (Eccles. 4:5). At first, it's hard to see the relevance of this gruesome picture for our lives. *When do we ever have time to fold our hands or take it easy? If only!* Recently, an earnest, young, aspiring pastor asked a pastor's wife what she and her husband did for fun in their free time. "We don't have hobbies and holidays," the mom explained, laughing. "We have teenagers!" This wasn't a complaint, but a comment on reality. Moms of teenagers don't have much time to sit around. So how do busy moms or diligent students end up folding their hands in foolishness? The problem is not rest (a gift from God), but resting at the wrong time and in the wrong way.

Each day, God has prepared good works for us to walk in (Eph. 2:10), but sometimes we procrastinate and put the hard stuff off until tomorrow. Or, we waste time, indulging in social media instead of attending to the work in front of us. Whether it's counseling a child or scrubbing a toilet, starting a difficult conversation or making a complicated decision, we're all tempted to put off tasks that seem unpleasant, or to indulge in small distractions. But Solomon wants us to see that putting off our work is more unpleasant than the work itself. Laziness is incompatible with enjoyment. In fact, if there is "nothing better . . . than to . . . do good" (Eccles. 3:12), there may be few things worse than to neglect the work God has given us to do. Idleness, to paraphrase Derek Kidner, has far-reaching consequences: eroding our self-control, our grip of reality, our capacity to care for others, and in the end, even our self-respect.[5] Consumed with ourselves, we may unwittingly end up consuming ourselves.

## Gospel Math: Three Are Better Than Two Are Better Than One

"Two are better than one. . . . A threefold cord is not quickly broken" (Eccles. 4:9, 12). We're all familiar with this particular snippet from Ecclesiastes, having seen it printed on our share of wedding programs. But Solomon is *not* talking about marriage with God at the center (although that's a great thing!). These verses are actually about work and community. Working side-

*Consider: How might laziness be de-motivating your work? How might you be experiencing the consequences of idleness in your life?*

*Repent where necessary, and ask for the Holy Spirit's power to work diligently as unto the Lord.*

by-side with others, he says, is the better way to live. Solomon has a little more fun with math here: *one is better than two* when we are talking about quietness in our work, but *two is better than one* when it comes to company in our work—and three (or more!) is even better! Here's some math we can get excited about. We all agree life and work are more fun with close family and friends. The more the merrier!

"Two are better than one" he says, and three are even better than that, "because they have a good reward for their toil" (Eccles. 4:9, 12). Here's another pleasant surprise. After repeatedly insisting that the worker can gain nothing under the sun, Solomon acknowledges that there is some "good reward" to be found after all for all our toil (Eccles. 4:9). We can reap a bountiful harvest from our labors when we work *together*. Partnership leads to profit. But it isn't primarily financial profit Solomon is talking about here. Instead, he points our attention once again to the good things in life: enjoying God's blessings *with* and doing good *for* others. The profit is in the camaraderie, mutual support, encouragement, and benefit we can give one another along life's journey. The gain is not on the far side of the work, but in doing the work side-by-side.

### The Blessings of Care, Comfort, and Camaraderie

Life in a healthy church community is full of rich rewards (Eccles. 4:9–12). Solomon practically trips over himself to pile up all the perks of working together. First, you have the benefit of *assistance*: "If they fall, one will lift up his fellow"—alone you have no one to pick you up (Eccles. 4:10). Every week, the two of us observe the women in our church assist one another when someone needs lifting up. Even in the process of finishing this book, we have been lifted up by prayers and practical help from others.

Together in community, we all experience the good reward of *comfort*: "If two lie together, they keep warm"—alone you are cold (Eccles. 4:11). It's such a comfort to have a friend who listens to our fears and doubts and shares the strengthening truth of Scripture with us. And in a time of mourning, we can weep with those who weep and so share the comfort that we ourselves have received from God (Rom. 12:15; 2 Cor. 1:3–4).

Finally, together we have the security of *defense*: "Two will withstand"—alone you are easy prey (Eccles. 4:12). It's a dangerous world out there under the sun. We have enemies on all sides from the world, the flesh, and the devil, but two (or more!) can withstand, if they stand together. This is why we must always refuse to listen to gossip or slander, and we must stand by and defend those who are falsely accused.

Two is better, and three or more are better than that. Here in Ecclesiastes, Solomon provides a rich portrait of community and companionship. When we assist, comfort, and defend one another, we have good reward for our work.

### The Freedom to Get to Work

Quietness isn't freedom *from* work, but freedom to *get to work*. It looks like rolling up our sleeves with a smile and getting our hands dirty with our duties, tenaciously tending to our lot: our homes, our families, our churches and communities—not because we will gain anything from them, but because God has already given them to us as a gift! Quietness joyfully embraces the place we have already been given to tend and mend instead of pining or striving for different circumstances. When we rejoice in our work, we find rest in our work. We choose a handful of quietness by "perform[ing] the duties of . . . present circumstances," explains Burroughs. "I know nothing more effective for quieting a Christian soul and getting contentment than this, setting your heart to work in the duties of the immediate circumstances that you are now in."[6]

And so we must ask ourselves: Are we content with the work God has given us, and are we doing that work diligently? Do we have one hand of quietness or two hands of envy and striving after the wind? As per usual in Scripture, things are different than what we expect: the way up is down, the last shall be first, and one handful is better than two hands full. Less with quietness is more. Or as the apostle Paul put it, "But godliness with contentment is great gain" (1 Tim. 6:6). Truly, as Solomon said, to work quietly is the best way to live.

---

*"For we ourselves were once foolish, disobedient, led astray, slaves to various passions and pleasures, passing our days in malice and envy, hated by others and hating one another. But when the goodness and loving kindness of God our Savior appeared, he saved us, not because of works done by us in righteousness, but according to his own mercy, by the washing of regeneration and renewal of the Holy Spirit, whom he poured out on us richly through Jesus Christ our Savior, so that being justified by his grace we might become heirs according to the hope of eternal life."* TITUS 3:3–7

---

Guard your steps when you go to the house of God. To draw near to listen is better than to offer the sacrifice of fools, for they do not know that they are doing evil. Be not rash with your mouth, nor let your heart be hasty to utter a word before God, for God is in heaven and you are on earth. Therefore let your words be few. For a dream comes with much business, and a fool's voice with many words.

When you vow a vow to God, do not delay paying it, for he has no pleasure in fools. Pay what you vow. It is better that you should not vow than that you should vow and not pay. Let not your mouth lead you into sin, and do not say before the messenger that it was a mistake. Why should God be angry at your voice and destroy the work of your hands? For when dreams increase and words grow many, there is vanity; but God is the one you must fear.

ECCLESIASTES 5:1–7

10

# Live Carefully

SEVERAL YEARS AGO, Carolyn was coming into church on a rainy Sunday morning. She had on heels, a nice dress, and a coat. In a flash—for that's how these things happen—she found herself face down on the wet sidewalk. A young man pushing a stroller nearby saw her fall and rushed to her aid, anxious that she might have hurt herself. Carolyn laughingly assured him that she was fine, and he offered his arm to help her up. Pulling together her umbrella, her purse, and her dignity, Carolyn walked the few remaining steps into church very carefully.

Here in Ecclesiastes 5, Solomon tells us to walk carefully into church: "Guard your steps when you go to the house of God" (Eccles. 5:1). It isn't high heels or slippery sidewalks Solomon is concerned about; he is warning us to watch our words and our hearts on our way into church. Do not rush into the church service, he exhorts us. While we are to work industriously, we must come to church cautiously. That's be-cause, when we come to the house of God—in Solomon's day, the temple, and in our time, the church—we are coming into the presence of God.

## Learning to Tread Carefully

Imagine that you were given an audience with the Queen of England. You would no doubt arrive early—in fact, that's one of many rules of protocol. You would walk carefully toward her, being sure to have practiced your curtsy. And you would *never* turn your back on her on your way out. These guidelines and more you would carefully follow. Contrast that with the way we often casually cruise into God's presence each week. Maybe you got up late, and instead of a shower, you pulled your hair into a messy bun. During church your mind wanders to conversations you hope to have during fellowship time (*I wonder how her vacation went?*) or to what you are going to have for lunch (*Deli sandwich or a fresh salad?*). Maybe you rush out as soon as church is over to watch a sporting event or take an afternoon nap.

Solomon knows the slapdash way we are tempted to go to the house of God, the place where we have been called together to worship. Here he warns us to proceed with the utmost caution. You are coming into the presence of the Holy One. Guard your steps, or else you may slip. Be very careful when you come into God's glorious presence. "Guard your steps" is Solomon's way of picturing the fact that we need to guard the way or the manner in which we come to worship (Eccles. 5:1). In short, he says, we should be *quick to listen* and *slow to speak* in the presence of God.

First, he says: we must be *quick to listen* to God: "To draw near to listen is better than to offer the sacrifice of fools, for they do not know that they are doing evil" (Eccles. 5:1). To point out what is "better" is Solomon's favorite way of telling us how to truly live. Here he tells us that it is way better to listen in church than to be fools.

You see, when we come to church, we draw near to God himself. It is true that we come to sing praises to God too, but even more importantly, we come to *listen* to God's word preached. We come to listen to the words that God himself has "breathed out" (2 Tim. 3:16). His words are not *hevel* like our words; Scripture contains the sure, eternal, authoritative, and unchanging words of God. And on Sunday mornings, God has appointed the preacher as his spokesman to deliver his words to his people. Solomon, "the Preacher," urges us to listen up.

Listening, of the biblical kind, requires preparation and application. We prepare for all kinds of things the night before to get the children off to school or to get to work on time or to get a jump-start on a big house project. How much more should we prepare to draw near and listen to God? The young people in Puritan pastor Richard Baxter's church apparently spent *three hours* together on Saturday evening, just to prepare their hearts for Sunday morning![1] Your preparation need not take three hours, but consider: How can you prepare your heart and your home for church?

Preparation begins with prayer. Pray that God would help you to draw near to him, to listen to his word, to hear his voice, and to receive grace to obey. Prayerfully review the past week: Is there any unconfessed sin in your heart, or any person with whom you need to be reconciled? Consider needs and requests for the week to come. When your heart is prepared to draw near to God, your thoughts will wander less and focus more on God's word. And if your church publishes the sermon text ahead of time, read and familiarize yourself with the passage. Practical preparation also aids your ability to listen well during church. Making plans the night before to get to church on time (or even a few minutes early) means you won't be so flustered and distracted when church starts. You will be on the edge of your seat, eager to listen to God.

But listening doesn't end with the preacher's closing prayer. Proper listening in Scripture does not occur until we *obey* what we hear. And so, instead of rushing out of church and into your week, take some time on Sunday afternoon or Monday morning to review the sermon and ask the Lord: What is one way I can listen by obeying this week?

*What is one way you can apply Solomon's admonition to "draw near to listen" (Eccles. 5:1) to God's word?*

## Check Your (Sinful) Attitude at the Door

Next, Solomon piles up the imperatives about taming the tongue in church. Not only should we be quick to listen, we should be *slow to speak*:

Be not rash with your mouth. (Eccles. 5:2)

Nor let your heart be hasty to utter a word before God. (Eccles. 5:2)

Therefore let your words be few. (Eccles. 5:2)

When you vow a vow to God, do not delay paying it. (Eccles. 5:4)

Let not your mouth lead you into sin. (Eccles. 5:6)

Scripture is replete with warnings about the tongue, but here Solomon tells us to be *especially* careful when it comes to the worship of God. To guard our "steps" (Eccles. 5:1) before we enter church means that we must guard our hearts (Prov. 4:23) and also guard our mouths (Prov. 21:23). We must not enter church having allowed sinful attitudes to enter our hearts, such as bitterness toward a fellow church member or selfish ambition for attention from others. We must not set foot in the church building without first setting a guard over our mouths from speaking words of pride, anger, criticism, or slander.

Think about the "words of [your] mouth and the meditation of [your] heart" at church last week (Ps. 19:14). Were they pleasing

*A command to obey and a prayer to pray:*

Know this, my beloved brothers: let every person be
quick to hear, slow to speak. (James 1:19)

Set a guard, O LORD, over my mouth;
keep watch over the door of my lips!"
(Ps. 141:3)

to God? How quickly did you drift from a focus on God to what
so-and-so was wearing? How many of your words before and after
church were hastily spoken and from an unruly heart? How free
did you feel to criticize your pastor's sermon or complain about
church leadership? Sadly, instead of being slow to speak, we are
all more likely to be quick to speak, quick to complain, and quick
to judge even (and sometimes especially) in church.

We are quick to speak (with authority) about what we think God is (or is not) doing. Quick to express an opinion about what another mom should or shouldn't do with her children. Quick to question and complain. Quick to criticize. We may dismiss hasty words and thoughts as harmless, but Solomon says they can be dangerous; so guard your steps by guarding your speech when you go to church.

### Vows to God

Slow to speak includes being slow to make vows to God: "When you vow a vow to God, do not delay paying it, for he has no pleasure in fools. Pay what you vow" (Eccles. 5:4). Because we moderns aren't given to making formal vows—except at weddings—we aren't sure of the immediate application of this verse. But while we may not "vow" in an official way, we do make commitments and promises at church, often rashly, to do such and such for God. We promise to "do better" this week at trying to break a pattern of sin. We promise God that we will read our Bibles every day or pray more often. We pledge to give a certain amount of money to the church. We promise the pastor that we'll jump in and help in a certain ministry. And then, almost before we have left the church building, we forget what we said we would do. The demands of the week rush in, and we fail to remember that we made promises *before God*. The next Sunday rolls around, and we make our excuses: "Oh, I'm sorry, Lord, but you know how busy my week was!" So for starters, suggests Solomon, it is better to just keep your mouth shut and not vow anything at all (Eccles. 5:5). But if you do make a vow to God, you had better keep it and right quick.

In fact, if you don't pay your vows to God right away, you might as well not bother doing any other work during the week, for God will oppose your work: "Why should God be angry at your voice and destroy the work of your hands?" (Eccles. 5:6). Again, reality check. If you are fond of promising God that you'll work for him and then leaving church to spend all week working for yourself, God may hinder all your industrious work. You do not want that, says Solomon. Trust me.

---

*"Whereas the prophets hurl their invective against the vicious and the hypocrites, [Solomon's] target is the well-meaning person who likes a good sing and turns up cheerfully enough to church; but who listens with half an ear, and never quite gets round to what he has volunteered to do for God."*[2] DEREK KIDNER

---

Why should we be slow of speech? In answer, Solomon delivers a smackdown of sorts: "For God is in heaven and you are on earth" (Eccles. 5:2). God is up there, and we are down here. And because God is in heaven, he discerns our thoughts from afar, and he knows the words on our tongues before we say them (Ps. 139:2, 4). Let your words be few because every one of them is before God. "If we are tempted to write this off as a piece of Old Testament harshness," advises Derek Kidner, "the New Testament will disconcert us equally with its warnings against making pious words meaningless, or treating lightly what is holy (Matt. 7:21; 23:16; 1 Cor. 11:27). No amount of emphasis on grace can justify taking liberties

*Are there any vows or commitments you have made to God and other people that you need to fulfill?*

with God."[3] Just ask Ananias and Sapphira (see Acts 5:1–11). And so, concludes Solomon, "God is the one you must fear" (Eccles. 5:7). Here, at almost the halfway mark of his book, Solomon reminds us once again what true life is all about: the fear of the Lord.

*"The blood of Jesus his Son cleanses us from all sin. If we say we have no sin, we deceive ourselves, and the truth is not in us. If we confess our sins, he is faithful and just to forgive us our sins and to cleanse us from all unrighteousness."* 1 JOHN 1:7–9

A good name is better than precious ointment,
  and the day of death than the day of birth.
It is better to go to the house of mourning
  than to go to the house of feasting,
for this is the end of all mankind,
  and the living will lay it to heart.
Sorrow is better than laughter,
  for by sadness of face the heart is made glad.
The heart of the wise is in the house of mourning,
  but the heart of fools is in the house of mirth.
It is better for a man to hear the rebuke of the wise
  than to hear the song of fools. . . .
Consider the work of God:
  who can make straight what he has made crooked?

In the day of prosperity be joyful, and in the day of adversity consider: God has made the one as well as the other, so that man may not find out anything that will be after him. . . .

. . . It is good that you should take hold of this, and from that withhold not your hand, for the one who fears God shall come out from both of them.

Wisdom gives strength to the wise man more than ten rulers who are in a city.

Surely there is not a righteous man on earth who does good and never sins.

Do not take to heart all the things that people say, lest you hear your servant cursing you. Your heart knows that many times you yourself have cursed others.

All this I have tested by wisdom. I said, "I will be wise," but it was far from me.

ECCLESIASTES 7:1–5, 13–14, 18–23

11

# Live Wisely

THROUGHOUT ECCLESIASTES 7, Solomon strings together what
may at first glance look like a row of random proverbs and nug-
gets of practical wisdom. (Did he copy and paste from his other
work?) Despite appearances, Solomon is never random. He is
making a cohesive point. Be realistic: be realistic about life, and
be realistic about the people you do life with.

## What If Prosperity Is a Curse and Adversity a Blessing?

Solomon puts all of life in two categories and suggests a wise response
to each: "In the day of prosperity be joyful, and in the day of adversity
consider" (Eccles. 7:14). Is it a day of prosperity? Smile. Is it a day of
adversity? Think. Once again, the New Testament comes to mind,
particularly James 5:13, where the brother of Jesus repeats Solomon's
counsel: "Is anyone among you suffering? Let him pray. Is anyone
cheerful? Let him sing praise."

Which kind of day is it for you today? For many of us, it is
a *day of prosperity*. We have food and shelter and church and

friends and family; we have coffee and books and a comfy chair to enjoy them in. If God the giver withdrew even one of these gifts, we would not have it anymore. So rejoice and be glad in this day of prosperity, for this is the day the Lord has made (Ps. 118:24).

It's that simple, but we don't always view it that way. Instead of receiving God's blessings with thankfulness, we overthink them. We attach erroneous and flattering interpretations to them, such as: "God must be really happy with my performance as a Christian to bless me like this," or "This blessing must mean that God supports this venture," or "If I do it this way the next time, then God is sure to bless me again." However, if we make our prosperity the proof of God's pleasure in us, we will find ourselves bewildered and despondent when the day of adversity comes. As one author explains: "Prosperity may be a camouflaged curse. . . . Adversity may be the means by which God is bringing great blessing. . . . All situations are not what they appear."[1]

Prosperity in Scripture is not the sole indicator of God's pleasure. In fact, at times the evil person seems to prosper most. So instead of analyzing our prosperity or making it the bellwether of God's pleasure, Solomon tells us to simply enjoy it. Receive it as a good and perfect gift, "coming down from the Father of the heavenly lights, who does not change like shifting shadows" (James 1:17 NIV). God is good, and he does good (Ps. 119:68). *All the time.* His pleasure in us is because we are in Christ his Son with whom he is well pleased. Receive the day of prosperity with joy and *don't* overthink it.

On the other hand, some of us have the jitters about prosperity. Blessings make us nervous and uncomfortable. You see, we've experienced enough of life under the sun to know that everything Solomon says is true enough: it's brief, baffling, and bad. We're so accustomed to adversity and so pessimistic about the future, that a day of prosperity smells highly suspicious to us. "Not to be trusted!" we declare. "Bound to end in disaster!" Days of prosperity are, to our minds, little more than bad omens. But this response only exposes our ongoing attempts to control and comprehend life. In a twisted kind of way, we think that if we decide now that today (and tomorrow and the next day) are going to be days of adversity, then we can do better damage control. Or we think we can calculate God's next move and get a jump-start on our response. But the result of this kind of wrong-headed thinking is that we not only worry when bad things happen, but we also worry when good things happen. And so, we end up worrying most of the time.

Now, it's true: tomorrow might be as bad as you think it's going to be. It could even be worse. Life is hard, says Solomon, and only gets harder. But it's also possible that tomorrow might be better than you imagine. It may be a day of prosperity. Because you cannot manipulate or predict what tomorrow will hold, Solomon tells us there's nothing for it but to simply rejoice. Don't spend all your good days *and* your bad days in misery. When things are good, be glad. This is not a shallow suggestion to make life bearable. It's a command. When your husband gets a better job or your child obeys, when you have five minutes by yourself with a rich cup of coffee, or when you have great fellowship with a family from church, rejoice. Not only does it make life more pleasant, it's also the only way to truly live. So how do we live well on a good day? Smile, easily and often. Sing songs of praise to God. Being joyful isn't a personality trait, it's a Christian virtue. "In the day of prosperity *be joyful!*" (Eccles. 7:14). Don't be happy-go-lucky, but do be happy-in-God.

*List some ways you are prospering right now.*

_____

_____

_____

_____

*How can you obey the command to be joyful in the day of prosperity?*

_____

_____

_____

_____

_____

_____

_____

_____

What about the *day of adversity?* True to form, Solomon's advice is unexpected. James's counsel, "Is anyone among you suffering? Let him pray" (James 5:13), we get: prayer seems an appropriate Christian response to suffering. But Solomon tells us to "consider" (Eccles. 7:14)—to ponder and meditate, to think a lot. Christians are not called to merely grit their teeth and bear hardship, neither should we try to escape reality. Rather, we must consider and interpret our suffering *biblically.* We must think straight about crooked days.

Solomon tells us *how* to think about adversity. When we suffer, we should meditate on the truth of God's inscrutable sovereignty: "God has made the [day of adversity] as well as the [day of prosperity], so that man may not find out anything that will be after him" (Eccles. 7:14). In other words, consider the fact that God is in control *and* that God has not made us privy to his future plans. He has made today with our adversity, just as he made yesterday with our prosperity. Same God. Same control. Same compassion. Same mystery. It's all him. He's made it, only he doesn't always tell us what it means. As Solomon puts it, we cannot find out anything that will be after us. We cannot predict, and we cannot even fully prepare for life's twists and turns. But although the day of adversity may be incomprehensible to us, it fits perfectly into God's wise and loving plan. While suffering may be out of our control, God is managing every moment for our good and his glory. We may not see *what* he is doing, but we are supposed to consider *that* he is doing it.

Why do we need to be exhorted to consider God's sovereignty? Because when bad things happen, we often try to figure them out. Sometimes we presume that the day of adversity means that God must be opposing our efforts, or we suppose our troubles will only go from bad to worse. Maybe we try to guess what good things God might bring out of this difficulty, long before he's ready to bring them out. One seminary professor describes his experience of trying to predict what God was doing: "There are times in life when I have stood on my tiptoes and looked over the wall, and it seemed to me I saw the pattern forming. I thought it was full and complete. And then something happens and it all breaks apart. And I'm cast back on the sovereignty of God again."[2]

The wise woman, says Solomon, doesn't try to predict the outcome of adversity; instead, she considers the sovereignty of God and she is comforted. There is, in fact, no comfort like knowing that God is in control. The same God who plans every day of prosperity allots every day of adversity. We cannot know what will come tomorrow, but we already know who *made* tomorrow and how we should respond. Be joyful, consider God, and live well.

### Sinners Gonna Sin, So Don't Be Surprised

Solomon also wants us to be realistic about people. In short, people are sinners: "Surely there is not a righteous man on earth who does good and never sins" (Eccles. 7:20). Remember where we are, Solomon urges us. We're "on earth," where life is outside our ability to manage or fix and is often tricky to figure out. The same is true in relationships: people are also difficult to fix or figure out, and Solomon wants us to be realistic about ourselves and others. Sinners are going to sin. So he suggests, "Do not take to heart all the things that people say, lest you hear your servant cursing you. Your heart knows that many times you yourself have cursed others" (Eccles. 7:21–22). Realistic expectations about people will spare us a lot of heartache.

*How does considering the sovereignty of God bring comfort in the day of adversity?*

In these verses, Solomon targets a particular area of trouble for those of us living under the sun, for few things hinder our enjoyment of life more than the people we do life with. We're surprised by slights and blindsided by criticisms. "Can you *believe* what she said about me?" we cry to our husbands (and heaven help them if they answer "Yes"!). "Now that I know what she *really* thinks about me . . ." we fume, as if this changes everything. We get into what Jonathan Edwards calls a "ruffle or tumult"[3] over people's unkind or ungracious comments. But if we are going to live well, we can't live this way. If we want to enjoy life, then we need to be realistic about the way people really are and so avoid getting all in a tangle about the things they say.

The wise woman will not "take to heart" other people's snubs, criticisms, or spiteful words. She'll keep the door of her heart closed and let their comments bounce back to the curb. She won't give these words hospitality in her heart because she knows they will only tear the place apart. Why should we let other people's complaints and criticisms go their merry way without taking them too seriously? Well, because the reality is, *sinners* are the ones doing the criticizing. Sinners are gonna sin and say stuff that is rude, unkind, and even untrue. That's how it goes here under the sun.

Your friend might get impatient and snap at you, or a woman at church might be envious and criticize you. At other times, you may just be in the wrong place at the wrong time, on the receiving end of your husband's frustration at someone else. A stranger may make a rude comment, not because you did anything, but because he is bitter at life and everyone. Being realistic about people—their sinful tendencies and difficult circumstances—helps us remain composed and serene no matter how uncharitable their words may be. This works the other way as well. We should not be quick to take to heart all the flattering things people say about us either. As Charles Spurgeon humorously puts it, "Those who praise us are probably as much mistaken as those who abuse us."[4] If we take to heart everything that people say—whether complimentary or critical—we are not living wisely with others.

## A Humbling Truth

But honestly, other people aren't the only problem. Solomon is quick to point out that we are sinners (and that we know it) too. "Your heart knows that many times you yourself have cursed others" (Eccles. 7:22). Acknowledging our own guilt keeps us humble. Have you ever made a critical comment about your boss? Have you criticized your husband or complained about your children? Have you ever made a disparaging remark about another woman at church? Sadly, we have criticized others many times. Far from condoning gossip, criticism, or slander, this verse forces us to admit that we have all engaged in sinful speech.

So how do we follow Solomon's wise advice for living realistically with others (and ourselves)? First order of business: don't pay attention to the sinful things that people say. Don't even listen. Block it all out. Charles Spurgeon again, keying off of Solomon, says: "You cannot stop people's tongues, and therefore the best thing is to stop your own ears and never mind what is spoken."[5] Don't take it to heart. Second, and more importantly, we should pay attention to what God says. We should keep God in view in all our dealings with other people. Whatever challenges in community we encounter or whatever good rewards in marriage or friendship we experience, God the giver has given us both. He uses all times and seasons in our relationships—the difficult and the delightful—to teach us to fear him and walk in his ways under the sun.

Being realistic about our lives and about the people in our lives is not always easy to do. This is why we need daily doses of realism from Ecclesiastes. We need to read this book regularly to remind ourselves what life and people are truly like and how to truly live. Living with an Ecclesiastes mindset will turn us into truly happy, hopeful realists.

*"I pray the Lord to give you a gentle and loving spirit towards all men, and a practical conviction that grace alone has made you to differ. It is easy to acknowledge this in words, but it is a great thing to act suitably to such an acknowledgement."*[6]  JOHN NEWTON

*We need God's grace to be gentle and loving toward others and humbly realistic about ourselves. Therefore let us ask God for grace, which he delights to give.*

_____

_____

_____

_____

_____

_____

_____

Go, eat your bread with joy, and drink your wine with a merry heart, for God has already approved what you do.

Let your garments be always white. Let not oil be lacking on your head.

Enjoy life with the wife whom you love, all the days of your vain life that he has given you under the sun, because that is your portion in life and in your toil at which you toil under the sun. Whatever your hand finds to do, do it with your might, for there is no work or thought or knowledge or wisdom in Sheol, to which you are going.

ECCLESIASTES 9:7–10

# 12

# Live Joyfully

WHEN THEIR CHILDREN WERE LITTLE, Carolyn and CJ instituted "Family Night" once a week in the Mahaney home. Carolyn would cook a meal everyone liked (as in *not* CJ's favorite chicken livers), and she planned special games and outings. They had Olympic competitions tossing ping-pong balls into bowls of water and ran relay races with toothpicks and Life Saver candies; they went for surprise trips to Baskin-Robbins ice cream; they played board games in the winter and played at the park in the summer. Always, there was a book to be read aloud. Family night was on Monday evenings, and even when the girls got old enough to drive and make plans of their own, it was a fixture in the week. Monday night, the Mahaneys made sure to celebrate together.

Celebration, says Solomon here in Ecclesiastes 9, must be the "prominent tone"[1] of our lives. Back in Ecclesiastes 8, Solomon strongly encouraged joy: "And I commend joy, for man has nothing better under the sun but to eat and drink and be joyful" (Eccles. 8:15), but now he outright commands it:

Go, eat your bread with joy, and [go] drink your wine with a merry heart. (Eccles. 9:7)

Let your garments be always white. (Eccles. 9:8)

Let not oil be lacking on your head. (Eccles. 9:8)

Enjoy life with the wife whom you love. (Eccles. 9:9)

Whatever your hand finds to do, do it with your might. (Eccles. 9:10)

Notice the number of imperatives in these verses: no fewer than six. And so we arrive again at joy. Perhaps because most of the first two chapters of Ecclesiastes are so unremittingly gloomy, people don't often think of Ecclesiastes as a joyful book and thus don't read it very often. But as we now know, one of Solomon's main goals is to teach us how to enjoy life under the sun. He takes enjoying life very seriously and so should we.

Like a mother prodding her child—"Don't be shy! Go have fun with the other kids!"—Solomon prods us to enjoy life. In fact, he insists on it. *Go*, get going already! Enjoy your life! Many of us are reluctant to enjoy life, even with a good shove from Solomon. If we find ourselves enjoying something even a little bit, our consciences go off and we start to worry that it's wrong. Maybe our church background emphasized asceticism, or perhaps we feel obligated to meet the needs of everyone around us. For whatever reason, many of us have a vague sense that only hard or unpleasant tasks are pleasing to God.

A friend of Carolyn's recently retired from a ministry job serving pastors' wives, and she admitted that she felt guilty for enjoying a quiet hour with a book in the middle of the afternoon. Solomon would say that she should feel guilty for *not* enjoying that quiet hour with a book, if it is a gift from God. When God gives us gifts to enjoy, it is in fact our duty to enjoy them. He is not more pleased with us if we refuse godly pleasures. And what are godly pleasures? J. I. Packer helpfully explains:

> If pleasure comes unsought, and if we receive it gratefully as a providential gift, and if it does no damage to ourselves or to others, and if it involves no breach of God's laws, and if the delight of it prompts fresh thanksgiving to God, then it is holy. But if the pursuit of one's pleasure is a gesture of egotism and self-indulgence whereby one pleases oneself without a thought as to whether one pleases God or anyone else, then, however harmless in itself the pleasure pursued may be, one has been entrapped by what the Bible sees as the pleasures of the world and of sin (see Luke 8:14; 2 Tim. 3:4; Titus 3:3; Heb. 11:25; James 4:3; 5:5; 2 Pet. 2:13). The same experience—eating, drinking, making love, listening to music, painting, playing games, or whatever—will be good or bad, holy or unholy, depending on how it is handled. In the order of creation, pleasures as such are meant to serve as pointers to God.[2]

Solomon speaks peace to the consciences of those who feel guilty about enjoying God's good gifts in God's time: "God

*What godly pleasures can you receive gratefully as a providential gift from God and enjoy for his glory?*

has already approved what you do" (Eccles. 9:7). Repeat this liberating line to your conscience the next time the devil accuses you of laziness or licentiousness while taking pleasure in what God has provided. By enjoying God's good gifts, we humbly receive them as from his hand. Far from displeasing God, our enthusiastic enjoyment honors him as the giver of all good things. It is a holy enjoyment.

### Giving Thanks for All Things, All Day, Every Day

Solomon's not just insisting that we celebrate occasionally, like schools take off for government holidays. He wants joy to be a way of life for all of life. Our garments are "always" to be white—the ancient form of festive dress (Eccles. 9:8); oil should "not . . . be lacking" from our head—to keep our skin and hair glowing (Eccles. 9:8); and he insists we enjoy our marriages "all the days of [our] vain life" (Eccles. 9:9). We are even to do our work with great enthusiasm, "with your might" (Eccles. 9:10). Nothing is to be half-hearted or half-baked. In other words, all of life is to be conducted in a celebratory manner. A festive atmosphere should pervade every aspect of our lives.

It's worth considering for a moment: Can we truly say that we have a festive spirit? Would our friends and family describe us as a happy woman? Often we compartmentalize our enjoyment. We think of work and sacrifice as our service to God and pleasure as "me" time. But Solomon wants us to think differently: if all of life is a gift from God, then all of life should be a celebration and enjoyment of those gifts.

Often we look for enjoyment outside the gifts God has given to us. We think that pleasure is to be found in getting out of the house for an evening of fun or in disconnecting from life for a while in order to recharge. If only we can escape from our responsibilities and relationships for a bit, *then* we can enjoy ourselves. But Solomon tells us that the greatest joys are not "out there" or "someday" but right here, right now, waiting to be celebrated: food and drink shared with family and friends, laughter and love in a godly marriage, festive clothes and scented soaps, and yes, even the joy of washing your dishes and shining your floors with all your might.

*What are some gifts right in front of you that you have failed to enjoy because you are longing for gifts "out there"?*

_____

_____

_____

_____

_____

_____

_____

_____

## Eat Up and Keep Sending the Thanks Up

This lovely ideal of a celebratory life may seem out of reach for the tired mom whose toddler has spaghetti sauce caked on her face from lunchtime, or the haggard mother of teenagers who is caring for her sick mother-in-law too. But remember, Solomon the realist is the one giving orders here. Mr. Unhappy Business himself commands us to be happy! Don't wait to get life under control before you celebrate—eat, drink, and be merry because the sovereign God has ordained your joy. Don't wait until your troubles go away to enjoy life—enjoy life right through to the other side of your troubles. Because all things are full of unutterable weariness, take a shower and put on something nice. All the days of your vain life under the sun are nothing more than a breath—*hevel*—so be happy on this day of vanity. The way over the hurdles and through the hedges of life is to celebrate. In the simple, daily ritual of family meals, God's most resplendent gifts of joy under the sun can come together for an hour or so of refreshment and delight. Here you can gather your family in one place with the husband "whom you love" (Eccles. 9:9) and "eat your bread with joy and drink your wine with a merry heart" (Eccles. 9:7). At family dinner we take a deep breath from our toil; we sit in our chairs and simply enjoy, no one striving after success, no one chasing the wind. Nothing is achieved here, but oh, so much is received. Is it any wonder that Psalms describes the home of the godly as having children like olive shoots *around the table* (Ps. 128:3)? Or that our Savior ordained that his sacrifice for our sins would be remembered by *a meal* (Matt. 26:26–28)?

Nothing fancy is needed to be festive. A meat, a vegetable, some pasta, glasses of water with ice floating cheerily, familiar jokes your kids like to tell, friends to join in on the fun from time to time—and you have enjoyments that Solomon himself says are the best life has to offer. Not every family dinner is idyllic; toddlers have to be taught to stay in their chairs, milk spills, a hormonal teenage daughter sheds some tears, the biscuits burn on the bottom. But the merry-making magic of this ritual is in its regularity, not in its perfection.

In addition to family meals, every one of us—regardless of our family situations—can enjoy God's good gifts of food and fellowship through the celebratory practice of hospitality. When we show hospitality to one another, we not only celebrate God's ordinary gifts, we imitate, however faintly, his extraordinary generosity. Over time, family meals and hospitality drape happiness like a garland over our home and church life under the sun.

---

*"There is no occasion when meals should become totally unimportant. Meals can be very small indeed, very inexpensive, short times taken in the midst of a big push of work, but they should always be more than just food. Relaxation, communication and a measure of beauty and pleasure should be part of even the shortest of meal breaks."*[3] EDITH SCHAEFFER

---

## Thanksgiving in Marriage for Marriage

Enjoying life is not a solo sport. You must do it with others. In fact, back in Ecclesiastes 4, Solomon paints a dismal portrait of the "one person who has no other . . . yet there is no end to all his toil, and his eyes are never satisfied with riches" (Eccles. 4:8). The single woman is not in view here, but rather the selfish person who refuses to give herself to others. Contrast the person here in Ecclesiastes 9 who enjoys life *with* others, and most especially in the marriage relationship. This verse addresses the husband, but it applies to us wives as well. We are to enjoy life all the days of our vain lives *with* the husband we love. The verse doesn't tell us merely to put up with him, but to *enjoy* life with him. We should enjoy being with him, working with him, and reaping the fruit of our labors with him. Enjoyment in marriage isn't something you hope you get lucky in; it's something you choose to receive as a gift from God. Marriage was given for joy. As Martin Luther is commonly quoted as saying, "Let the wife make her husband glad to come home and let him make her sorry to see him leave."[4]

## Thanksgiving: The Sweetener for the Bitter Things in Life

A protest rises in our throats: What about times when long-term hardships or relational conflicts wear us down? For example, what about the woman whose husband cannot hold down a good job or whose teenager is angry and morose? Here again, enjoyment is the key. By doggedly delighting in God's good gifts, a godly woman can lighten her husband's load, soften her child's heart, and lift her own spirits as well. It is hard to keep sinning and sulking when you live with a woman who persists in celebrating life, Solomon style, no matter what. Vanity is turned to victory when we fight futility with joy. "Even though life's puzzles and enigmas could easily sour us towards life," acknowledges one author, "wise people celebrate life today as God's good gift to be enjoyed, and they are alert to ways in which to do that. This does not mean being *less* serious about the pains of life, but it is being *more* celebratory about the pleasures God gives to us in life."[5] Serious trouble calls for more serious celebration in our everyday lives.

"Pleasure," writes J. I. Packer, "is divinely designed to raise our sense of God's goodness, deepen our gratitude to him, and strengthen our hope as Christians looking forward to richer pleasure in the world to come."[6] Festivity is not frivolous. It raises, deepens, and strengthens our faith and hope in God the giver. It makes life under the sun not only bearable, but boisterous. Meals together fortify us for life's trouble, marriage mollifies life's sharp trials, and God the giver prepares us to celebrate in his presence for all eternity. So what are you waiting for? Go and get celebrating already!

---

*And day by day, attending the temple together and breaking bread in their homes, they received their food with glad and generous hearts, praising God and having favor with all the people. And the Lord added to their number day by day those who were being saved.* ACTS 2:46–47

---

Cast your bread upon the waters,
for you will find it after many days.
Give a portion to seven, or even to eight,
for you know not what disaster may happen on earth.
If the clouds are full of rain,
they empty themselves on the earth,
and if a tree falls to the south or to the north,
in the place where the tree falls, there it will lie.
He who observes the wind will not sow,
and he who regards the clouds will not reap.

As you do not know the way the spirit comes to the bones in the womb of a woman with child, so you do not know the work of God who makes everything.

In the morning sow your seed, and at evening withhold not your hand, for you do not know which will prosper, this or that, or whether both alike will be good.

ECCLESIASTES 11:1–6

13

# Live Boldly

WHEN CAROLYN WAS NINETEEN, she decided to leave her home in Bradenton, Florida, in order to attend a Bible college in Dallas, Texas, for a year. She had already resigned her job and finished packing up her apartment when, just a few days before she was set to move, she met CJ. It was love at first sight. Ten months later, they were married and moved into a little apartment in Silver Spring, Maryland. One year after that, their first child, Nicole, was born. Just goes to show, you never know what's going to happen next.

That's Solomon's point, once again, here in Ecclesiastes 11. He's fond of repeating himself because he knows it will take a while for the truth to sink in. If there's one thing we can be certain of, he tells us, it is that we live in an uncertain world. Sometimes the unpredictable is exciting—like when Carolyn met CJ—and other times it can be disorienting and even difficult. But this is the way life is under the sun. Solomon not only wants us to see the way life truly is, he teaches us how to deal with it. Here in these verses, he trains us how to cope, but more than that, how to thrive, in a life where nothing is certain or predictable.

### Even If You Know More Than a Fourth Grader, You Still Don't Know That Much

Multiple times in this passage, we find some variation on the phrase *"you do not know."* No matter how hard we hit the books and no matter how much life experience we have behind us, there is still a whole lot more we *don't* know about life.

*"You know not what disaster may happen on earth"* (Eccles. *11:2).* Even today as we write this chapter, rescue workers are searching for survivors of a condominium collapse in Miami, Florida. You do not know what disaster may happen at any time or place on earth.

*"You do not know the work of God who makes everything"* (Eccles. *11:5).* You cannot explain God's providence in the times and seasons of your life so far, or predict what he may call you to do in the future.

*"You do not know which [effort] will prosper"* (Eccles. *11:6).* The weather, the economy, and other people are all unpredictable. You cannot know for sure which path in life will lead to the most success.

### Success Is Not Certain but Failure Is Not Final

No matter how many times we read "you do not know," it doesn't always sink in. We think that if we set smart goals, study up on how to achieve the perfect body or successful kids or a great retirement or a thriving small business, then as long as we do it right, we can be confident in a good outcome. We assume that life is like a vending machine: we can put in a dollar and get out a candy bar. But success in life doesn't work that way. Solomon reminds us (over and over!) that we do not know what will happen. Success is *not* guaranteed. And no amount of wisdom on our part can ensure a specific result. We might put in a dollar and get nothing, or we might get two candy bars for the price of one. But we just don't know! We don't know which of our efforts will prosper and which will fail. We don't know *the work of God.*

Sometimes, though, we look ahead and predict failure. In cases such as these, we may hesitate or even refuse to move forward in life unless we have some sort of guarantee of a good outcome. Maybe we've stepped out and taken a risk before, only to have it all end in disaster. *I'm not making that mistake again,* we say to ourselves. Or we may have watched a friend take a dead-end path, so we'd rather sit on the curb. Perhaps after surveying the field, we realize we'll be mediocre at best, and so we prefer to sit the game out rather than play a supporting role. Rather than predict failure before we even try, Solomon tells us not to predict anything at all. We cannot be sure whether this or that venture will fail, or whether "both alike will be good" (Eccles. 11:6).

### Show Some Spirit and Give from Your Gifts

If we can't predict the outcome of anything we do, where does that leave us? Solomon tells us exactly how we should respond to the unpredictability of life. We should truly live! We should bravely, exuberantly, freely run into the risks and uncertainties

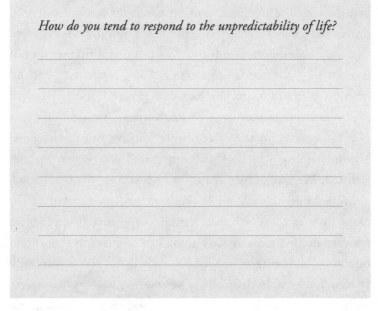

*How do you tend to respond to the unpredictability of life?*

of life instead of shrinking back. As Derek Kidner puts it, "The true response to uncertainty is a redoubling of effort. . . . The very smallness of our knowledge and control, the very likelihood of hard times, so frequently impressed on us throughout the book, become the reasons to bestir ourselves and show some spirit."[1]

Rather than myopically pursue a certain outcome or hold back in fear of failure, we should show some spirit. We should take risks. "Cast your bread upon the waters, for you will find it after many days" is a reference to putting your investment on a ship bound for a distant port (Eccles. 11:1). In other words, instead of stockpiling your resources, send them out! Don't hold back because you think something might go wrong. Instead, courageously invest your life resources, and someday there will be a return (just not in the time or way you can predict).

"Give a portion to seven, or even to eight, for you know not what disaster may happen on earth" (Eccles. 11:2). Give to seven—the number of completeness—and then look around for who else you can give to. Give everything you think you can, and then give some more. As one author writes,

> Some people will say, "The future is uncertain, so eat dessert first. You may not live to eighty, so why save and save and save? Spend now and enjoy it while you can." But here's what Ecclesiastes is saying: "The future is uncertain, so give your dessert away. Give it away. Sit loose to life by giving your life away. Sit loose to your possessions by giving them away."[2]

We cannot get anything out of this life; everything we have is a gift from God the giver. Now, Solomon urges us to imitate God in our generosity. Life is a gift, so *give*. And then give some more. How do selfish sinners become fearless givers, even of their very lives? By living for our Savior, who gave his life for us: "And he died for all, that those who live might no longer live for themselves but for him who for their sake died and was raised" (2 Cor. 5:15).

Like Jesus Christ, we should live with fearless generosity. Fearless generosity is not for the select few who have time and money to spare. It is for every one of us. It means we should gather up whatever resources God has given us today, and give them away to people right in front of us: our family, our church, and our neighbors. We don't know what is going to happen tomorrow or next year, so we should give away all we can of our time, money, gifts, and talents *today.* Our friend Dawn is a talented and creative baker who makes the best almond-laced sugar cookies you've ever eaten. Rather than use her considerable talents to promote her own reputation or make loads of money, Dawn donates many evenings after work, and most weekends, to cook for church events. All proceeds from her successful small business—baked goods for holidays and special occasions—go directly to our church's building fund. Dawn had knee replacement surgery this past year, and even though she's still in pain months later, she hasn't slowed down. She isn't sure how many years she can keep up this pace, but her enthusiasm never flags. She's busier than ever training young women to serve the church in hospitality. Dawn lives each day with fearless generosity.

*Who is an example to you of fearless generosity? Tell her. Then consider: How can you emulate her example?*

_____

_____

_____

_____

_____

_____

_____

## Spend Your Days

Life is unpredictable. Carolyn could not have guessed how her life would radically change one summer day in 1974; neither do we know what the next season holds, or even tomorrow for that matter. So how do we respond to life's unpredictability? Give your life away today. Rather than holding out for a particular outcome, spend your time and energy on gospel work. Rather than holding on to your resources, give away your money and your talents while you still can. The New Testament echoes Solomon's wisdom: "Remember this," Paul tells us. "Whoever sows sparingly will also reap sparingly, and whoever sows generously will also reap generously" (2 Cor. 9:6 NIV). While we live, let us *truly* live, with fearless generosity.

*God has richly provided us with everything to enjoy. How can you imitate him and be rich in good works—fearlessly generous—toward others this week?*

*"As for the rich in this present age, charge them not . . . to set their hopes on the uncertainty of riches, but on God, who richly provides us with everything to enjoy. They are to do good, to be rich in good works, to be generous and ready to share, thus storing up treasure for themselves as a good foundation for the future, so that they may take hold of that which is truly life."* I TIMOTHY 6:17–19

The end of the matter; all has been heard. Fear God and keep his commandments, for this is the whole duty of man. For God will bring every deed into judgment, with every secret thing, whether good or evil.

ECCLESIASTES 12:13–14

## 14

# Live Fearfully

WHEN NICOLE WAS LITTLE, she accompanied her parents on several ministry trips to London, England. For some reason she came back from one of these trips repeating a single phrase in her seven-year-old imitation of a posh British accent: "It doesn't mattah." It was cute while it lasted, which was only a couple of weeks. But here, in the final verses of Ecclesiastes, Solomon tells us the opposite is true: It *does* matter. In fact, everything matters. It couldn't matter more.

## Absolutely Right

Ecclesiastes is a book of absolutes. Whether speaking positively or negatively, Solomon speaks absolutely. He insists that "*all* is vanity" and that "there is *nothing* better" than to enjoy life (Eccles. 12:8; 2:24) His conclusion here, about what matters, is true to form: "The *end* of the matter; *all* has been heard. Fear God and keep his commandments, for this is the *whole* duty of man. For God will bring *every* deed into judgment, with *every* secret thing,

*The Proverbs 31 woman exemplifies the hard-working wisdom of Ecclesiastes. Take some time to study Proverbs 31:10–31. Where do you see a resemblance?*

_____

_____

_____

_____

_____

_____

_____

*How can you model your life after this woman who feared the Lord and filled her post?*

_____

_____

_____

_____

_____

_____

_____

whether good or evil" (Eccles. 12:13–14). *All* has been heard. All has been heard about all of life under the sun, from "a time to be born" to "a time to die" (Eccles. 3:2). All has been heard on how to find success (you won't), where to get satisfaction (not here), what kind of work we have to do (unhappy business), and how it's all going to end (badly). All has been heard, and Solomon's conclusion is this: All is vanity. All is *hevel*. Under the sun we will never be in control or be in the know. We will never be able to get ahead, fulfill our dreams, prevent disasters, or wrestle life down into something manageable. We cannot figure out what it all means or what will happen on the earth. We cannot fix it. It's all beyond us, all too much for us. Absolutely all of it.

All our frustrations in life—*all of them!*—are meant to lead us to one place, or rather to one person: God. All our questions, all our confusion, all our problems are to compel us to fear him and obey. To keep God in view and to keep his commands is our whole duty for our whole lives. It is at once shorthand and comprehensive, taking in everything. It is the *end* of the matter for all that matters. As Martin Luther writes:

> The main point in this book is, that there is no higher wisdom on earth under the sun than that every man should fill his post industriously and in the fear of God, not troubling himself whether or no his work turn out as he would fain have it, but contenting himself, and leaving the ordering of all things great and small entirely to God. . . . And thus a man should not worry and question and trouble himself how things will or should turn out in the future, but think within himself—God has entrusted me with this office, with this work, and I am

resolved to discharge it diligently: if my counsels and plans do not succeed as I expected, let God dispose, ordain, and rule as He will.[1]

Fill your post and fear God. That's how to truly live your merest breath of a life. You do not know what will succeed, and you do not know what will fail. So fear God. Keep him in view. For those of you who are young and don't know what to do with your lives: fear God and keep his commandments. For those of you who have lived longer and been surprised by the way life has turned out: fill your post and keep fearing God. If we demand answers to all our "why?" questions or try to control what's going to happen next, we will drive ourselves into despair. But if we ask: "How can I fear and obey God right now?" there will always be an answer.[2] There will always be a way forward.

## The Grand Simplifier

Solomon has spent twelve chapters mapping out the terrain of life under the sun and teaching us how to navigate it well. He's explained what it looks like to fear God and obey him with our money, our work, our marriages, our food, and our drink. And here at the end, he brings them together in beautiful summation. How do we live in the fear of the Lord and obedience to him? We laugh hard and give generously. We enjoy every day we have with our husbands. We make frequent feasts to celebrate God's goodness with our families and friends. We pay close attention to what we say and little attention to what others say about us. We go to church faithfully and guardedly. We keep our vows.

Enjoy life. Worship God. Sing while you clean, laugh while you feast, listen while you worship, consider while you suffer. Fear and obey. This is the whole dangerous, delightful duty that we have been given here under the sun. So simple. So joyful. So glorious. True life awaits the woman who, by the power of the Holy Spirit, fears God and keeps his commandments.

As we told you at the beginning of this book, Ecclesiastes has changed our lives, and it continues to renew and transform our days. Life hasn't turned out like we thought, but Ecclesiastes has taught us how to enjoy life through good days and bad. We're not so surprised when things go wrong (it's an Ecclesiastes world, after all!), and yet we are more amazed at the beautiful sovereignty of our God (Eccles. 3:11). Whether our seasons are full of pain or pleasure, we can receive God's gifts and fill our posts. Every day may be different, but the way to live every day is the same. "Fear God and keep his commandments" is the grand simplifier of our lives.

---

*"These two points—the Preacher pronounces to contain the whole of man—not his duty only, but his whole happiness and business —the total sum of all that concerns him—all that God requires of him—all that the Savior enjoins—all that the Holy Spirit teaches and works in him."*[3] CHARLES BRIDGES

---

## Living in Light of Judgment Day

Before we go, Solomon has one final point to make. Now that all has been heard and our whole duty has been made clear, Solomon tells us *why* we should fear God and obey. If Ecclesiastes 12:13 tells us the way to really live under the sun, then verse 14 tells us the really good reason to live that way. Why are we to fear God and keep his commandments? Why does it matter? "For God will bring every deed into judgment, with every secret thing, whether good or evil" (Eccles. 12:14).

While it's true that almost nothing we do will be remembered under the sun, everything we do will be recorded for the final judgment. God will judge every good deed and every evil deed. Our good works—even the ones we have long forgotten about—will be remembered and rewarded on that day. And our secret sins, the ones we thought we had hidden so well? Each and every private thought or act will be brought out into the open. Think about it. One day we will give an account for every envious effort or selfish striving, *and* for every act of fearless generosity or gracious enjoyment of God's gifts. Every deed, whether good or evil, secret or public, will be brought into judgment by God.

"But wait," you may be asking, "I thought the final judgment was for *unbelievers*?" Rest assured, you are not the only one with that question. "Judgment Day is an event that the church has nearly implied to be a no-show opportunity for believers washed in the Saviour's blood," acknowledge two commentators on the book of Ecclesiastes. However, "an acquittal comes only after charges have been made. God's very glory and honour, his perfect expectations and perfect love, require that the fullest extent of our sin be realized . . . in order to appreciate but a fraction of his grace."[4]

For Christians, the day of judgment will be a humbling recounting of the evil things we have done under the sun. But it will also be a glorious receiving of the mercy and grace of God.

*I tell you, on the day of judgment people will give account for every careless word they speak, for by your words you will be justified, and by your words you will be condemned.* MATTHEW 12:36–37

What punishment we deserve. And what forgiveness we have received! All because of the blood of Christ. At the final judgment, all who have trusted in Jesus and his life, death, and resurrection will be acquitted of all their sins under the sun. But there's more: we will also be rewarded for every good deed—every quiet work or joyful service—that was done in obedience to Christ. Your good deeds may not be remembered here under the sun (many of them won't even be noticed), but if you are a Christian, then every one of them will be rewarded in heaven. Judgment day highlights our eternal gratitude for the grace of God in forgiving all our evil deeds and rewarding all our good deeds.

*It is the Lord who judges me. Therefore do not pronounce judgment before the time, before the Lord comes, who will bring to light the things now hidden in darkness and will disclose the purposes of the heart. Then each one will receive his commendation from God.* 1 CORINTHIANS 4:4–5

And so, the final judgment *is* the reason to fulfill our whole duty: to fear God and keep his commands. Paul, writing to *Christians*, reaffirms the importance of the day of judgment as a motivation to fear God and obey: "We make it our aim to please him. For we must all appear before the judgment seat of Christ" (2 Cor. 5:9–10). As Derek Kidner puts it so well: "It kills complacency to know that nothing goes unnoticed and unassessed, not even the things that we disguise from ourselves. But at the same time it transforms life. If God cares as much as this, nothing can be pointless."[5] Here is the life-transforming truth of the final judgment for those who are in Christ. Everything will be judged. Everything matters. Nothing is meaningless under the sun.

In the end, the message of Ecclesiastes is this: what you do with your vain life under the sun truly matters. It matters because of what God has done. "He has made everything beautiful in its time. . . . Whatever God does endures forever" (Eccles. 3:11, 14). His works and his judgments are eternal. In Christ, our works too will last forever. Our work done in the fear of God and obedience to his word is not vanity. It is *more* than a breath. It will remain. It will matter. It will endure. And so, we find the true life wisdom of Ecclesiastes in 1 Corinthians 15:58: "Therefore, my beloved brothers, be steadfast, immovable, always abounding in the work of the Lord, knowing that in the Lord your labor is not in vain."

*"Grant, O Lord, that we may live in thy fear,*
*die in thy favour, rest in thy peace,*
*rise in thy power, reign in thy glory;*
*for thine own beloved Son's sake,*
*Jesus Christ our Lord."*[6] WILLIAM LAUD

# Notes

## Introduction

1. J. I. Packer, "J. I. Packer: How I Learned to Live Joyfully," *Christianity Today*, September 9, 2015, https://www.christianitytoday.com.
2. Packer, "J. I. Packer: How I Learned to Live Joyfully."
3. Martin Luther, quoted in E. W. Hengstenberg, *A Commentary on Ecclesiastes* (Eugene, OR: Wipf and Stock, 1998), 32.

## Chapter 1: Life Is Uncontrollable

1. Robert Alter, *The Wisdom Books: Job, Proverbs, and Ecclesiastes: A Translation with Commentary* (New York: W. W. Norton & Co., 2011), 340.
2. Alter, *The Wisdom Books*, 346.

## Chapter 2: Life Is Wearisome

1. Iain Provan, *Ecclesiastes, Song of Songs* (Grand Rapids, MI: Zondervan Academic, 2001), 56.
2. Douglas Sean O'Donnell, *Ecclesiastes* (Phillipsburg, NJ: P&R, 2014), 29.

## Chapter 3: Life Is Unhappy

1. Derek Kidner, *The Message of Ecclesiastes* (Downers Grove, IL: IVP Academic, 1984), 15.
2. Martin Luther, quoted in Jaroslav Jan Pelikan, *Luther's Works Ecclesiastes, Song of Solomon and the Last Words of David/2 Samuel 23:1–7* (St. Louis: Concordia College, 1971), chap. 5.
3. Paul David Tripp, *Suffering: Gospel Hope When Life Doesn't Make Sense* (Wheaton, IL: Crossway, 2018), 31.

4. Thomas Watson and Hamilton Smith, *Extracts from the Writings of Thomas Watson*, Illustrated ed. (Fincastle, VA: Scripture Truth Publications, 2009), 43. Scripture in this quote is from the King James Version.

Chapter 4: Life Is Grievous

1. Jeffrey Meyers, *Ecclesiastes through New Eyes: A Table in the Mist* (Monroe, LA: Athanasius Press, 2007), 60.
2. John Calvin, quoted in Jonathan Gibson, *Be Thou My Vision: A Liturgy for Daily Worship* (Wheaton, IL: Crossway, 2021), 130–31.

Chapter 5: Life Is Enjoyable

1. Derek Kidner, *The Message of Ecclesiastes* (Downers Grove, IL: IVP Academic, 1984), 35.
2. Isaac Watts, "Joy to the World," Timeless Truths Free Online Library, accessed October 12, 2021, https://library.timelesstruths.org.

Chapter 6: Life Is Well-Timed

1. Derek Kidner, *The Message of Ecclesiastes* (Downers Grove, IL: IVP Academic, 1984), 38.
2. Jeremiah Burroughs, *The Rare Jewel of Christian Contentment* (London: Banner of Truth, 1964), 111–12.
3. David Gibson, *Living Life Backward: How Ecclesiastes Teaches Us to Live in Light of the End* (Wheaton, IL: Crossway, 2017), 54.
4. Jonathan Edwards, *Charity and Its Fruits: Christian Love as Manifested in the Heart and Life*, ed. Tryon Edwards (Milwaukee, WI: Banner of Truth, 1969), 80.
5. Burroughs, *The Rare Jewel of Christian Contentment*, 111–12.
6. Daniel C. Fredericks and Daniel J. Estes, *Ecclesiastes & the Song of Songs* (Downers Grove, IL: IVP Academic, 2010), 117.

Chapter 7: Life Is Incomprehensible

1. J. I. Packer, *Knowing God*, 20th Anniversary ed. (Downers Grove, IL: IVP Books, 1993), 106.
2. John Piper, "God Is Always Doing 10,000 Things in Your Life," *Desiring God* (blog), January 1, 2013, https://www.desiringgod.org.
3. Ellen Vaughn, *Becoming Elisabeth Elliot*, Illustrated ed. (Nashville, TN: B&H Books, 2020), 111.
4. Os Guinness, *God in the Dark: The Assurance of Faith beyond a Shadow of Doubt* (Wheaton, IL: Crossway, 1996), 170.
5. Vaughn, *Becoming Elisabeth Elliot*, 111.

6. Martin Luther, quoted in Jaroslav Jan Pelikan, *Luther's Works Ecclesiastes, Song of Solomon and the Last Words of David/2 Samuel 23: 1–7* (St. Louis: Concordia College, 1971), chap. 3.

7. Jeremiah Burroughs, *The Rare Jewel of Christian Contentment* (London: Banner of Truth, 1964), 66.

*Chapter 8: Live Faithfully*

1. C. S. Lewis, "Learning in War-Time," *The Weight of Glory and Other Addresses* (San Francisco: HarperSanFrancisco, 1980), 62–63.

2. Derek Kidner, *The Message of Ecclesiastes* (Downers Grove, IL: IVP Academic, 1984), 36.

3. Jeffrey Meyers, *Ecclesiastes through New Eyes: A Table in the Mist* (Monroe, LA: Athanasius Press, 2007), 64.

4. Elisabeth Elliot, *Suffering Is Never for Nothing* (Nashville, TN: B&H Publishing, 2019), 45–46.

5. David Gibson, *Living Life Backward: How Ecclesiastes Teaches Us to Live in Light of the End* (Wheaton, IL: Crossway, 2017), 37.

6. Quoted in Justin Taylor, "Do the Next Thing," The Gospel Coalition (blog), October 25, 2017, accessed October 13, 2021, https://www.thegospelcoalition.org.

*Chapter 9: Live Industriously*

1. Jeremiah Burroughs, *The Rare Jewel of Christian Contentment* (London: Banner of Truth, 1964), 45.

2. Derek Kidner, *The Message of Ecclesiastes* (Downers Grove, IL: IVP Academic, 1984), 45.

3. Rebecca Konyndyk DeYoung, *Glittering Vices: A New Look at the Seven Deadly Sins and Their Remedies*, 2nd ed. (Grand Rapids, MI: Brazos Press, 2020), 52.

4. Joseph Epstein, *Envy: The Seven Deadly Sins* (New York: Oxford University Press, 2003), 1.

5. Kidner, *The Message of Ecclesiastes*, 46.

6. Burroughs, *The Rare Jewel of Christian Contentment*, 51–52.

*Chapter 10: Live Carefully*

1. J. I. Packer, *A Quest for Godliness: The Puritan Vision of the Christian Life* (Wheaton, IL: Crossway, 1990), 241.

2. Derek Kidner, *The Message of Ecclesiastes* (Downers Grove, IL: IVP Academic, 1984), 52.

3. Kidner, *The Message of Ecclesiastes*, 53.

### Chapter 11: Live Wisely

1. Douglas Wilson, *Joy at the End of the Tether: The Inscrutable Wisdom of Ecclesiastes* (Moscow, Idaho: Canon Press, 1999), 75.
2. Haddon Robinson, "The Message of Ecclesiastes," *Preaching Today*, accessed October 13, 2021, https://www.preachingtoday.com.
3. Jonathan Edwards, *Charity and Its Fruits: Christian Love as Manifested in the Heart and Life*, ed. Tryon Edwards (Milwaukee, WI: Banner of Truth, 1969), 80.
4. C. H. Spurgeon, *Lectures to My Students: Complete & Unabridged* (Grand Rapids, MI: Zondervan, 1954), 326.
5. Spurgeon, *Lectures to My Students*, 321.
6. John Newton, *Wise Counsel*, ed. Grant Gordon (Carlisle, PA: Banner of Truth, 2009), 15.

### Chapter 12: Live Joyfully

1. Daniel J. Estes, *The Message of Wisdom: Learning and Living the Way of the Lord* (London: Inter-Varsity Press, 2020), 178.
2. J. I. Packer, "Pleasure Principles," *ChristianityToday*, November 22, 1993, accessed October 13, 2021, https://www.christianitytoday.com.
3. Edith Schaeffer, *The Hidden Art of Homemaking* (Wheaton, IL: Tyndale, 1985), 123.
4. "Quotes by Martin Luther," Grace Quotes, accessed October 15, 2021, https://gracequotes.org.
5. Estes, *The Message of Wisdom*, 178.
6. Packer, "Pleasure Principles."

### Chapter 13: Live Boldly

1. Derek Kidner, *The Message of Ecclesiastes* (Downers Grove, IL: IVP Academic, 1984), 98.
2. David Gibson, *Living Life Backward: How Ecclesiastes Teaches Us to Live in Light of the End* (Wheaton, IL: Crossway, 2017), 125.

### Chapter 14: Live Fearfully

1. Martin Luther, quoted in O. Palmer Robertson, *The Christ of Wisdom: A Redemptive-Historical Exploration of the Wisdom Books of the Old Testament* (Phillipsburg, NJ: P&R, 2017), 272.
2. Adapted from J. I. Packer, *Praying the Lord's Prayer* (Wheaton, IL: Crossway, 2007), 14–15.
3. Charles Bridges, *Ecclesiastes* (Edinburgh: Banner of Truth, 1961), 310.

4. Daniel C. Fredericks and Daniel J. Estes, *Ecclesiastes & the Song of Songs* (Downers Grove, IL: IVP Academic, 2010), 251.

5. Derek Kidner, *The Message of Ecclesiastes* (Downers Grove, IL: IVP Academic, 1984), 107.

6. William Laud, quoted in Kidner, *The Message of Ecclesiastes*, 110.

# General Index

living boldly, 137–44
to show your spirit and give your
gifts, 139–42
and the things we do not know,
138
uncertainty of success and
failure, 138–39
living carefully, 103–111
learning to tread carefully, 104–6
living faithfully, 83–91
living fearfully (fear of the Lord),
147–54
in light of judgment day, 151–54
living wisely, 113–22
prosperity as a curse and adversity
as a blessing, 113–18
Luther, Martin, 17, 44, 78–79, 133
on Ecclesiastes, 149–50

Mahaney, Carolyn (author), 29, 34,
35, 57, 59, 76–77, 78, 83, 93,
103, 125, 137, 143
Mahaney, CJ, 57, 76, 125, 137
Margaret (Carolyn's mother), 34–35
marriage, thanksgiving in, 132–33
*Message of Ecclesiastes, The* (Kidner),
41, 61, 66, 84, 97, 110, 140,
154, 155n1, 156n1 (ch. 5),
156n1 (ch. 6), 157n2 (ch. 8),
157n2 (ch. 9), 157n2 (ch. 10),
158n1, 159n5
*More-with-Less* (cookbook), 93

O'Donnell, Douglas Sean, 37

Packer, J. I., 14, 15, 75, 127, 133
Paul, 101, 143, 153
on life as vanity, 26
on marriage and motherhood, 43
physical beauty, 24

"Pleasure Principles" (Packer), 127,
133, 158n2, 158n6
prayer, 88–89
preparation begins with, 105–6
prosperity, 113–16

quietness, 94, 100–1

relationships, 21, 23, 31, 33, 41, 65,
67, 118, 121, 129
complexities and complications
of, 68, 70–71
rest, 95, 97

Sapphira, 111
Schaeffer, Edith, 132
self-control, erosion of, 97
sinful attitudes, 107–9
sinners, 120–21
slander/false accusations, 23, 107
Solomon, 12, 14–15, 23, 25, 32,
35, 41, 43–44, 58, 80, 85–86,
90, 95, 99–100, 111, 117, 119,
137, 150
accomplishments of, 49–50
on God's gifts, 127–28
perspective of on life, 17
predictions concerning death,
52–53
policy of more with less, 93
on sinners, 120–21
on spending days wisely, 143
"under the sun" phrase, 29
wisdom of, 88
on the wise woman, 118
Spurgeon, Charles, 120, 121
*Suffering Is Never for Nothing*
(Elliot), 88, 157n4

thanksgiving, 128–29
and the celebratory life, 130–31

# Scripture Index

# Also Available from Carolyn Mahaney and Nicole Whitacre

For more information, visit **crossway.org**.